PRESE

Contents

Preface

Can it be said that the Church of Scotland is today satisfying the spiritual needs of the people of Scotland?

In all honesty, and however deeply it hurts, one is bound to give a negative answer. In so far as it offers any comfort it may confidently be said that Scottish Presbyterianism is not in such deep trouble as are some other denominations in these islands and overseas. It can be said too that in some Scottish parishes there are welcome signs of spiritual renewal and increased membership as a result of devoted work by ministers, elders and members. None can, however, deny that all is not well with the Kirk.

It is not that people in general have completely turned their backs on religion, for most acknowledge the existence of God. But belief in an after-life and the Christian concept of the life of here-and-now as a brief testing ground for eternity are not held sufficiently strongly to fashion belief and to determine conduct. Within the Church itself the Scriptures are not known as they should be, nor are the essentials of the Christian faith either fully understood or accepted.

This weakening of Christian conviction has inevitably led to a dwindling in the influence of the churches, alongside which has gone a great increase in the sphere of activity of the State. On every hand we hear demands that the State should do more in this or that field or should increase the spread of its authority still further. To vast numbers the State is seen as immeasurably more important than the Church.

In face of these challenges the reaction of the various churches has been hesitant and confused. There are those who pin their hopes on a union of the separate denominations, believing that an all-embracing Church would somehow provide an early solution for these urgent problems. There are others who would subordinate the preaching of the Word to the administration of the sacraments in the conviction that this would bring a resurgence of faith. Others again, while retaining the centrality of preaching, would tie it to some form of fundamentalism.

We all pray for a revival of faith, but we cannot foresee the form which it may take. In the past much devoted effort has gone into national campaigns of revival. This may be the way forward in the future or revival may well up from local sources. This little book is not concerned with modes of encouraging mission. It is concerned with the underlying structure and doctrine of the Church, within which revival takes place and which holds existing and new members. Too often change is lauded just because it is change. We need to decide what in our heritage should be preserved and developed and what should be discarded.

These are questions in which I, like many others, have an intense interest. I was born in Edinburgh and attended school and university in that city, although since the age of twenty-three I have lived and worked in London. You may ask, then, what concern all this is of mine – what title have I to write about the future of the Kirk? My answer would be threefold. First, I am a member of the London Scottish community (embracing St Columba's Pont Street and Crown Court) which remains faithful to the Church of Scotland. Second, the outsider often enjoys the best view of the game and, because of my geographical detachment, I have a view to put forward on what has been happening north of the border. And, third, the process of secularisation and the reaction to it of the churches have in various ways proceeded faster and further in England than in Scotland, so that there is a mass of English experience from which useful lessons are to be learned.

But the most valuable lessons will always be those learned from the history of our native land. The 350th anniversary of the National Covenant and of the Glasgow Assembly of 1638 is a good occasion for trying to discover what the past has to teach us in these matters.

Alexander Johnston

London, December 1987

I

Our Heritage

1638

Professor Wallace Notestein of Yale University in *The Scot in History* (1946) said that nothing is more important than religion in explaining the Scottish character. He was referring to the Reformed religion, Calvinist and Presbyterian, as finally established in 1690.

The strength of Calvinism lay in its deep roots. 'Rabbi' Duncan (1796–1870) put this provocatively when he said that there was no such thing as Calvinism. 'The teaching of Augustine, Remigius, Anselm and Luther were just pieced together by one remarkable man, and the results baptised with his name. Augustine taught and developed the doctrine of salvation by grace and the divine election; Remigius, particular redemption; Anselm, the doctrine of vicarious atonement; and Luther, that of justification by faith.'[1]

At the core of Calvin's teaching was his sense of God's greatness and of his scheme of salvation for the world. Calvinism represented a philosophy of history based on sounder grounds than Marxism. God had a slowly unfolding purpose to achieve on earth, through his people. They had to help to bring about the coming of God's reign on earth by combating evil and injustice. In 1539 Cardinal Sadolet wrote to the inhabitants of Geneva that they were imperilling their immortal souls by not returning to the Roman Catholic Church. Calvin's main argument in reply, in terms that were echoed later in the answer to the first question in the Shorter Catechism, was that the prime duty of a Christian was to glorify God and carry out his will. 'There is no man imbued with true piety who will not consider as feeble your long and laboured exhortation to zeal for the heavenly life, a zeal which keeps a man entirely devoted to himself and does not, even by one expression, arouse him to sanctify the name of God.'[2] There was a sense of organised action and discipline. This is the

Calvinism that created a sense of dedication and enthusiasm in so many countries, including Scotland – not the determinism arising from double predestination which is so often misrepresented as the essence of Calvin's teaching.

The scene was set in 1560 for the way in which the Reformed Church of Scotland would develop. *The Scots Confession* set out Reformed theology with freshness and directness. The *Book of Common Order* provided for simple forms of church services and for the singing of the metrical Psalms. *The First Book of Discipline* was notable for instituting the office of elder, elders being chosen by votes of the congregation and being given an effective voice in the government and discipline of the church. The Lord's Supper was to be celebrated four times a year in towns and less frequently in the country. For the full development of the presbyterian system, one has to wait for *The Second Book of Discipline* and later. *The Second Book of Discipline* also clearly set out what had been implicit from the start of the Scottish Reformation – that the church had an existence and authority independent of the state.

In 1592, after various reversals of fortune, the Church of Scotland seemed to be established as Reformed in theology and in form of service and presbyterian in church government. But James VI had formed the settled view that presbyterianism 'as well agree with the monarchy as God and the devil.' He gradually secured the introduction of bishops into the Church. In 1618 a packed Assembly at Perth agreed to the Five Articles which, *inter alia*, required the sacrament to be received kneeling, children to be presented to the bishop for confirmation at eight years of age and the observance of various holy days. James did not, however, attempt to abolish kirk sessions or presbyteries and abandoned a proposal to abolish general assemblies. In the country at large the Five Articles were frequently disregarded.

Charles I had none of his father's caution. Under the influence of William Laud, Archbishop of Canterbury, he was determined to rule the Church of Scotland and to introduce into Scotland the Anglo-Catholic practices which Laud was endeavouring to introduce in England. Canons were published in 1636, on the King's authority, based on the English model. Anyone who denied the King's supremacy in ecclesiastical causes was to be excommunicated. There was no reference to elders, kirk sessions, presbyteries or the General Assembly. There was no mention of deacons to handle financial matters, but only of deacons on the Anglican model as the lowest tier of the clergy. This was not episcopacy imposed on presbyterianism, as with James, but simple episcopacy.

What provided the spark for the conflagration was the *Scottish Prayer Book of 1637*, which was intended to introduce Anglo-Catholic practices into the public worship of the Church of Scotland. A royal proclamation required its observance. There followed the celebrated riot in St Giles on 23 August 1637 associated with the name of Jenny Geddes and a month later a more serious riot in Edinburgh on 25 September. The country-wide objections were that the prayer book was Romish, that it came from England and that it was being imposed on the church by the mere fiat of the King. The Scottish Privy Council was hopelessly divided. To prevent too many protestors swarming to the capital, the Council proposed that nobles, lairds, burghers and ministers should form committees or 'Tables', eventually consisting of four members each, to represent their interests. In November 1637, the Tables presented to the Privy Council a supplication against the use of the prayer book and for the removal of bishops from the Council.

Charles rejected these demands in the spring of 1638. The Tables, which came close to being an alternative Government, then decided to strengthen their position by securing the nation-wide signing of a national covenant. The National Covenant became a protest against innovations and was signed by all classes of the community.

The Covenant was skilfully drafted by a lawyer, Archibald Johnston of Warriston and a minister, Alexander Henderson, who emerged from parish work at Leuchars to give leadership to the Church. The Covenant was based on the so-called *Negative Confession* which had been prepared in 1581 when there were special fears about the activities of Roman Catholics. The *Negative Confession* endorsed *The Scots Confession of 1560* and went on to emphasise the points on which the Reformers disagreed with the Roman Church. *The Negative Confession* had been signed by James VI, the royal household and privy councillors. The signatories to the National Covenant pledged themselves to defend the true Reformed religion as set out in the Confession and to support the King in his preservation of the true religion, liberties and laws of the kingdom. The Covenant concluded with the signatories promising to keep within the bounds of Christian liberty and to be good examples of godliness, soberness and righteousness and of every duty they owed to God and man.

Because of the other difficulties which beset him at this juncture, Charles I had reluctantly to agree to a free Assembly and a free Parliament and to fix a date for both. Thus it came that a General Assembly met in Glasgow Cathedral on 21 November 1638 – the first Assembly since 1618.

With Alexander Henderson elected as moderator, the members of the Assembly from the start showed their determination to assert the independence of the Church in spiritual matters. To this the Kirk has remained deeply attached at all crucial points in its history. James VI had endeavoured to control the Church and to modify its government and worship in an Anglican direction. While he appointed bishops and claimed the power to regulate worship, he proceeded cautiously and used Parliament and packed assemblies to secure his ends. Charles I, on the other hand, made no pretence of using organs of ecclesiastical government and so precipitated conflict. When the Marquis of Hamilton, as high commissioner, saw the direction that the assembly was taking, and in particular the intention of a body containing elders to try the bishops, he dissolved the assembly in the King's name and declared that its continuance would constitute treason. He then withdrew, accompanied by two ministers and three elders. The assembly continued to sit and in due course fixed a date for the next meeting. The assembly tried the bishops for various offences, deposing all and excommunicating some, declared that six 'pretended' assemblies between 1606 and 1616 had no authority, condemned the *Canons*, *Scottish Prayer Book* and the Court of High Commission, abolished episcopacy and said that ministers should not be members of the Scots Parliament or accept civil office. No more emphatic declaration of the spiritual independence of the Kirk could have been made.

From 1638 onwards, the presbyterian form of church government became entrenched in the minds and hearts of the great majority of the members of the Scottish Church. In 1581 the General Assembly had established presbyteries and adopted the *Second Book of Discipline* which set out the presbyterian system of government. Thereafter James VI and Charles I had imposed various forms of episcopacy. The National Covenant was concerned with worship and doctrine rather than church government. It was the Assembly of 1638 which swept away the accretions since 1581 and set the Church of Scotland firmly on the presbyterian path. There was a flood of works justifying presbyterianism in the 1640s. Samuel Rutherford, George Gillespie, Alexander Henderson and others developed the case for presbyterianism with much learning and weighty argumentation. It was to presbyterianism that the Church returned in 1690 after the bitter experiences of 1660 to 1688. We now know what happened after 1638 and we treat the Glasgow Assembly as a step towards the overthrow of Charles I in the Civil War. The position must have seemed very different to the members of the Glasgow Assembly after the high commissioner's dissolution of the assembly and his declaration that its continuance would constitute treason. Charles was considering how to muster sufficient force to quell Scotland; and it required great courage and steadfastness in their beliefs for the leaders of the assembly to persevere in the course on which they had embarked.

In 1638 the place of the elder in the government of the Church was firmly established in the minds of presbyterians. Geneva had provided no clear guidance for the constitution of a general assembly covering a whole country. In the 16th century assemblies, there were representatives of shires and burghs who were not necessarily elders. The *Second Book of Discipline* endeavoured to secure that only 'ecclesiastical persons' (that is, ministers and elders) should vote at assemblies, but it is not clear that this was given effect to, though re-enacted in 1586 and 1597. The nobles and others with whom James VI packed his later assemblies were not necessarily elders. In the preparations for the 1638 Glasgow Assembly, the Tables required that an elder from each parish should attend the presbytery and these elders participated in the voting for ministers and elders to be sent as commissioners to the assembly. The bishops in a protest to the assembly said that in the past elders had never chosen commissioners for the assembly and 'only were sometimes called to assist in discipline and correction of manners'. (Clearly the bishops would have approved of the Panel on Doctrine's proposal in 1985 that elders should concentrate on service and pastoral care.) The question was argued to and fro between Edinburgh and London whether the high commissioner should say, before the assembly got to work, that it was not validly constituted because of the part played by ruling elders. The decision was that it would be dangerous to close down the assembly immediately. Where a small group wish to control a church, they dislike the idea of any real authority residing outside their ranks. Their prototype is Monseigneur Talbot, the friend of Cardinal Manning, who commented thus on the strong public support given by prominent Roman Catholic laymen to John Henry Newman:

> What is the province of the laity? To hunt, to shoot, to entertain. These matters they understand, but to meddle with ecclesiastical matters they have no right at all.

Mgr Talbot would not have enjoyed the Glasgow Assembly. As already indicated, the elders in many presbyteries had been responsible for the choice of ministers and elders for the assembly and at the assembly itself the elders were a powerful force.

The National Covenant and the decisions of the Glasgow Assembly were the result of a nation-wide enthusiasm for the Reformed faith, and these events fanned that enthusiasm still further. In part this was based on a dread of Roman Catholicism. Spain was feared and the Armada was still in the public mind. France had been lost to Protestantism and had a population several times that of Great Britain. The ferocious Thirty Years War was still being waged in Germany and its outcome was uncertain. No doubt political, social and economic issues entered into the calculations of many; but the dominant force was religious. Bishop Burnet in his *History of His Own Times* describes the ministers of this era in the west of Scotland:

> They used to visit their parishioners much, lived in great familiarity with them, and in matters of religion made them their partners as it were and companions. They were so full of the Scriptures, and so ready at extemporary prayer, that from thence they grew to practise extemporary sermons; and their method of preaching was so clear in raising points of doctrine out of the text, then proving these observations by reasons, and so showing the use that was to be made of the whole for instruction and terror and for exhortation and comfort, that the people could follow a sermon through every branch of it.

In another passage he describes the intimate knowledge that ordinary people had of the great issues facing the Church.

It can of course be said that the enthusiasm was excessive and expressed in terms that are unacceptable to modern ears. The Church of Scotland was the divine church which Christ 'made a fair bride to Himself'. Scotland was the new Israel, and Israel and Scotland were 'the only two sworn nations to the Lord'. Yet here was a force which, properly directed, the Church desperately needs today. It will neither be evoked by little groups working out ecclesiastical formulas nor by asking the Panel on Doctrine what we are supposed to believe. It has to come by widespread inculcation of Christian principles in the population at large and it will come from a resultant resurgence of belief, welling upward. It can legitimately be combined with pride in a form of church government that gives to every member the feeling that he or she shares in the running of the church. It was said in the past that the Scots were a homogeneous and practical people, so that all classes could unite in common opinions about religion, politics and social justice. If it is difficult to say this of politics, at least let us recover our homogeneity on other issues within the framework of our presbyterian church.

After 1638

It is an extraordinary fact that, in a violent age and in a rather turbulent nation, the Scottish Reformation, in spite of its revolutionary character, was carried through without killings in cold blood. Much sound and fury and some destruction of property but not bloodshed. In 1638 there were wild words and riots and it was said of the Glasgow Assembly 'not a gown among them but many had swords and daggers', but the year passed without bloodshed. Events after 1638 were different. There were merciless killings before the final settlement of 1690. The Civil War introduced a new dimension of violence. One has also to accept that the elements of compromise – never a feature that the Scottish mind finds particularly attractive – that existed in some of the earlier arrangements were lacking after 1638.

Again there had been little tendency to schism before 1638. The internal strength of the organisation based on kirk sessions and presbyteries discouraged breakaway tendencies. The innovations of James VI were either accepted unwillingly or not observed by those who disliked them; but no one left the church. The hardening of the lines of division and more effective central control led in due course to the schisms for conscience's sake which were a feature of the 18th century – sometimes too much conscience in matters that did not require damaging divisions.

How are we to rate the *Solemn League and Covenant* of 1643 and its attempt to secure a presbyterian church in England and Ireland? The Scottish Commissioners who pressed for this almost certainly believed that presbyterianism would be acceptable in England. They were probably misled into thinking that the warm welcome they received in London, despite their 'barbarous accents', reflected opinion throughout the country, which it did not.

The Covenanters, who were so sorely persecuted under Charles II and James VII, were of course staunchly presbyterian and wished to see presbyterian government in England and Ireland as well as in Scotland. But, as a recent study[3] has pointed out, for most covenanters the movement was primarily a struggle against state control of the Scottish Church. In this respect, they were in a line that stretched back to Andrew Melville and forward to the Secessions of the 18th century and to the Disruption of 1843. Lord Cockburn said of the Disruption: 'no spectacle since the Revolution reminds one so forcibly of the Covenanters'.

The Claim of Right, subscribed by the Scots Parliament in 1689, stated that 'prelacy and the superiority of any office in the Church above presbyters is and has been a great and insupportable grievance to this nation and contrary to the inclinations of the generality of the people.' The inclination of the generality of the people was based on the belief that presbyterianism was in accord with the New Testament and indeed there were those who argued that it was the only scheme of church government which had full scriptural support. In 1690, presbyterianism was finally established and the *Westminster Confession of Faith* approved as the public confession of the Church.

The 18th century is often represented as a time when enthusiasm and deep convictions ran low. Yet when Dr Samuel Johnson visited Scotland in 1773, he found on every hand Scots who defended vehemently their Calvinist and presbyterian church. Adam Smith, though not a member of any church, praised presbyterian ministers in *The Wealth of Nations*. 'There is scarce perhaps to be found anywhere in Europe a more learned, decent, independent and respectable set of men than the greater part of the presbyterian clergy of Holland, Geneva, Switzerland and Scotland'. And again 'The presbyterian clergy have more influence over the minds of the common people than perhaps the clergy of any other established church. It is accordingly in presbyterian countries only that we ever find the common people converted, without persecution, completely and almost to a man, to the established church'.

In the second reading debate on a Bill about religious tests for Chairs in Scottish universities Lord Macaulay said on 9 July 1845: 'All staunch presbyterians think that the flock is entitled, *jure divino,* to a voice in the appointment of the pastor, and that to force a pastor on a parish to which he was unacceptable is a sin as much forbidden by the Word of God as idolatry or perjury. I am quite sure that I do not exaggerate when I say that the highest of our high churchmen at Oxford cannot attach more importance to episcopal government and episcopal ordination than many thousands of Scotchmen, shrewd men, respectable men, men who fear God and honour the Queen, attach to this right of the people.'[4]

In the Disruption of 1843, one third of the ministers of the Church of Scotland gave up their livings rather than remain in a church which they saw as subject to State control. They were supported by a substantial proportion of the church members and all the overseas missionaries. Lord Jeffrey said 'I'm proud of my country: there is not another country upon earth where such a deed could have been done'.

Some years later, in 1872, Dean Stanley went north to Edinburgh to explain how misguided the Scots had been to attach importance to the issues which had led to the secessions from the established church in the 18th century and to the Disruption in the 19th century. Amid strong popular support, Principal Rainy answered in a rival series of lectures. The main thrust of his reply deserves to be quoted in full.

> The earnestness with which Presbyterianism was maintained was due to something else besides the confidence men had in their theoretical conclusions about Church government. Everything that is theoretically good and true has its practical witness in itself from which it receives daily confirmation. So was it with Presbyterianism. Presbyterianism meant organised life, regulated distribution of forces, graduated recognition of gifts, freedom to discuss, authority to control, agency to administer. Presbyterianism meant a system by which the convictions and consciences of the Church could constantly be applied by appropriate organs to her current affairs. Presbyterianism meant a system by which

quickening influence, experienced anywhere in the Church, could be turned into effective force and transmitted to fortify the whole society. Presbyterianism meant a system by which every one, first of all the common man, had his recognised place, his defined position, his ascertained and guarded privileges, his responsibilities inculcated and enforced, felt himself a part of the great unity, with a right to care for its welfare and to guard its integrity. From the broad base of the believing people, the sap rose through Sessions, Presbyteries, Synods, to the Assembly, and thence descending diffused knowledge, influence, organic unity through the whole system. Yes, Presbyterianism is a system for a free people that love a regulated, a self-regulating freedom; for a people independent, yet patient, considerate, trusting much to the processes of discussion and consultation, and more to the promised aid of a much-forgiving and a watchful Lord. It is a system for strong Churches – Churches that are not afraid to let their matters see the light of day – to let their weakest parts and their worst defects be canvassed before all men that they may be mended. It is a system for believing Churches that are not ashamed or afraid to cherish a high ideal and to speak of lofty aims and to work for long and far results, amid all the discouragements arising from sin and folly in their own ranks and around them. It is a system for catholic Christians who wish not merely to cherish private idiosyncracies, but to feel themselves identified with the common cause while they cleave directly to Him whose cause it is. Our fathers felt instinctively that the changes thrust upon them threatened to suppress great elements of good – not mere forms alone, but the life which those forms nourished and expressed. When Episcopacy shall have trained the common people to care, as those of Scotland have cared, for the public interest of Christ's Church, and to connect that care with their own religious life, as a part and a fruit of it, then it may afford to smile at the zealous self-defence of Scottish Presbyterianism.'

Over the centuries, there have been secessions from the Church of Scotland and from the Church of England. The seceding bodies in Scotland remained presbyterian, indeed usually seceded in order to preserve their presbyterian heritage as they understood it. The seceding bodies in England dropped episcopacy, having found, as it has been put, that 'the new wine of religious revival could not be contained in the old bottles of an episcopalian system'.

The leaders of the Church in the early part of this century were all sound presbyterians – John White, Alexander Martin and many others. Professor G D Henderson extolled the virtues of presbyterianism in the many books that he wrote on the subject. In *The Presbyterian Churches*, published in 1928, James Moffatt, better known for his translation of the Bible, set out the services that the presbyterian churches had rendered to the furtherance of the Christian religion. He described presbyterianism as belief in the apostolic and catholic Church as governed by presbyters. The constitutive principles which he set out may be summarised as follows:

a) the parity of ministers, by which none has any superior status in relation to the others,

b) the parity of teaching elders (ministers) and ruling elders, so that ruling elders, as representatives of the membership, take an equal part with ministers in the government of the church and

c) the unity of the church, not simply in faith and order, but in a graduated series of church courts which express and exercise the common authority of the church as a divine society.

He had also something to say about the incipient ecumenical movement:

> While a Church like the Presbyterian Church is tempted by its self-consciousness to exagerate and stiffen the statement of its characteristics in controversy, it may be prone to whittle them away in the opposite mood of warm sympathy with the spirit and aims of some Christian organisation in its neighbourhood. Now, nothing is gained by showing a sectional or insular temper in any division of the Christian Church; but *a Church is a Church, not an amorphous association floating on the tides of undenominationalism.*

Even in the dry bones of Cox's *Practice and Procedure of the Church of Scotland*, of which successive editions have been published up to 1976, there breathes a deep love of presbyterianism. Let us trust that the revision now under way preserves it.

Impact of ecumenism

The present century saw the development of the ecumenical movement. We shall have more to say on this anon, but here we are concerned with its impact on the Church of Scotland.

Anglicanism has tended to see itself as the *via media* to which all should conform in the search for unity. Although its own orders were not accepted as valid by the Roman Catholic Church, Anglicanism abandoned the acceptance of presbyterian orders it had shown in the early 17th century, and has not been prepared to accept as valid a church which did not embody the 'historic episcopate'. So far as the Church of Scotland is concerned, the history of ecumenism in the last fifty years is largely the history of efforts by ecumenists to get the Church to accept, in the cause of church unity, that its presbyterian organisation should be departed from and by implication that a church without bishops in the historic succession has never been a true church. However the point may be disguised, the validity of presbyterian orders lies at the root of the question. If they are valid in the eyes of episcopal churches, then there is no obvious need to make changes in the constitution of the Church of Scotland in order to achieve inter-communion. How far the Church of England is prepared to go in claiming that a church without bishops is not a true church was illustrated as recently as 1984 when a proposal came before the Church of England Synod that the Church of South India should be admitted to full communion with the Church of England. This was turned down because the Church of South India still had four aged ministers, never likely to leave India, who had not been ordained by a bishop.

Following informal discussions over a number of years, the General Assembly in 1932 agreed that a conference on church unity should be held between the Church of Scotland, the Church of England, the Episcopal Church in Scotland and the Presbyterian Church of England. As Dr Andrew Herron reminds us in his book *Record Apart,* Principal W M Macgregor pleaded in vain with the Assembly not to accept an invitation at that stage to engage in conversations with the Episcopal Church. 'Are they prepared to recognise us as in some full sense constituent members of the Catholic Church of the Lord Jesus Christ? They doggedly and continuously refuse or evade that decision'. He foretold that nothing would be achieved. The first fruits were brought before the General Assembly of 1933, when Dr Archibald Fleming of St Columba's, Pont Street, London, who had first-hand acquaintance with Anglican claims, successfully moved that 'any agreement with regard to the orders and sacraments of the conferring churches can be based only on the recognition of the equal validity of the orders and sacraments of both churches and of the equal standing of the communicants and of ordained ministers in each'. In his speech in the Assembly

Dr Fleming said that Church of Scotland pulpits were open to every Anglican divine and that the way to the Lord's Table lay unobstructed to every Anglican communicant. But the Church of Scotland would never surrender the validity of its ministry and sacraments. 'Let us get out of our minds the unscholarly interpretation of the Lord's prayer for unity which implies that unity means uniformity'. Talks continued, but without much progress: and then the Second World War came.

During the Second World War, the 'Reports of the Commission for the Interpretation of God's Will in the Present Crisis', and more particularly the 1943 report, dealt with the divisions in Christendom. Stress was placed on the need for closer understanding and co-operation between the different branches of the Church. 'It must be recognised, however, that co-operation in urgent common tasks is one thing and the attainment of some form of institutional unity quite another .... When the return of peace re-establishes easy communications between the nations, the World Council, in close association with the International Missionary Council, will be the focal point in shaping the approach of the Churches to the world, and will yet further develop policies of united action among them.'

Since the end of the war, interest has lain in the resistance of the bulk of the ministers and members of the Church of Scotland to attempts by influential ministers, attracted to the ecumenical movement, to abandon presbyterianism.

After the war, there were further discussions between the Church of Scotland and the Church of England about closer relations. A report was issued in 1951 which dealt with some short-term problems and envisaged a study of the kind of modifications in the two church systems which might be requisite in the context of 'the hoped-for reintegration of Christendom'. This led to discussions between representatives of the Church of England, Church of Scotland, Episcopal Church in Scotland and Presbyterian Church of England. It has been a matter of adverse comment that the Church of Scotland contingent contained eleven theological professors and ministers and no elder other than the procurator of the church.[5] The report that resulted, commonly known in Scotland as the *Bishops Report*, was published in 1957. Its main recommendation was that the Church of Scotland should appoint bishops who would preside over presbyteries – 'bishops-in-presbytery'. They would be consecrated by the laying on of hands by bishops from episcopal churches and thus be within the apostolic succession as understood by Anglicans. Bishops would be members of the General Assembly, 'without constituting an upper house within it, although decisions on doctrinal matters might well have to require their consent'. The eldership was to be studied by the Church of England and the Episcopal Church in Scotland.

There was immediately an uproar in Scotland at this proposed departure from the presbyterian system. Professor Gregor Smith, who had returned to a Divinity Chair in Glasgow after many years in the South, was surprised to find that the report filled the news and correspondence columns of the Scottish newspapers and that at political meetings, tea parties, and all manner of informal occasions it was the subject of animated and often acrimonious discussion. The Professor noticed with surprise that the publications of the signatories of the report and their friends bore the imprint of the Church of Scotland's own press, although he had no doubt that most members of the Church were ready to reject the whole report out of hand. 'No bishops' was the sum of their cry.[6]

The 1958 Lambeth Conference did not help by showing a lack of understanding of the Scottish situation and little interest in the eldership. The General Assembly of 1959 rejected the Bishops Report as unacceptable because it implied a denial of the Catholicity of the Church of Scotland and of the validity and regularity of its ministry within the Church Catholic.

The Church of England did not make any official pronouncement on the Bishops Report which it obviously regarded as simply bringing the Church of Scotland into line with the Church of England in church government and other matters. In England, the Scottish opposition to bishops was attributed to a campaign by the *Scottish Daily Express* and even today Anglicans assume that a dislike of episcopacy is based on folk-memories of unhappy times in the 17th century. The idea that members of the Church of Scotland could be strongly attached to presbyterianism as a system of church government has never penetrated Anglican thinking, in so far as any serious thought is devoted to Scottish affairs. Much less has it occurred to them that there are those who, on conscientious grounds, are opposed to the doctrine of the apostolic succession of bishops. To a presbyterian the Church abides, not because the ministry abides, but primarily because the Word of God abides. Believing that the ministry is the ministry of the Word, a presbyterian finds the continuity of the ministry and of the Church primarily in the Word itself that 'liveth and abideth forever', rather than in any human element. Yet the Bishops Report[7] spoke of the apostolic succession as something 'required' by presbyterians.

Discussions continued between representatives of the Church of England, the Church of Scotland, the Episcopal Church in Scotland and the Presbyterian Church of England. The result was a report entitled *Anglican-Presbyterian Conversations*, published in 1966. The authors might think that they could dispose of denominational differences, but they accepted that nationalism was a nut that they could not crack. The aim, as in the Bishops Report, was to be a Church of England and a Church of Scotland, separate but in full communion with each other. The report contained nonsenses such as that there should be a united church 'which would include both episcopalian and presbyterian essentials', but it recognised more soberly than the Bishops Report the difficulties in the way of organic unity. To that extent it was by implication an unfavourable indictment of the Scottish divines who had signed the Bishops Report. However it firmly established the Anglican position – for there to be complete intercommunion, the only kind of church north of the border which would be accepted would be an episcopal church.

So far as Scotland was concerned, attention was then focused on the Multilateral Conversation, begun in 1967, between the Church of Scotland, Churches of Christ, Congregational Union, Episcopal Church, Methodist Church and the United Free Church. The Conversation produced Controlling Principles to guide schemes of union and these were accepted by the General Assembly in 1969 but had a mixed reception in presbyteries. As the Inter-Church Relations Committee observed in 1974: 'It is disconcerting to realise that the welcome given to the Controlling Principles by the General Assembly of 1969 implied so little engagement in the mind of the Church'.

In 1972, the Multilateral Conversation produced a scheme for the introduction of superintendents into the Church of Scotland. A majority of presbyteries rejected this idea outright. The Inter-Church Relations Committee reported in 1974 that the failure to spell out the answerability of superintendents and their relationship to the courts of the Church was a major stumbling block, that their status in relation to bishops of other communions at present belonging to the historic episcopate also aroused suspicion and that there had been opposition to the surrender of parity in the ministry. Ever-hopeful, the Committee proposed that the deliverance of the 1974 Assembly should be to the effect that any proposal for the appointment of superintendents 'would require to be very specific in regard to the duties, authority, selection, terms of office and ordering of such persons'. Under the leadership of Dr Andrew Herron, the Assembly would have none of this and the deliverance, as passed, described the proposal as 'unacceptable to the Church of Scotland'.

Meantime in 1969–70, a scheme for union between the Church of Scotland and the Congregational Union was rejected by a majority of Church of Scotland presbyteries and by a majority of Congregational Union congregations. In 1971, a proposal that the Episcopal Church should become a non-territorial synod within the Church of Scotland was rejected by the Episcopal Church and never came before the General Assembly. A scheme worked out between 1972 and 1978, by which the Methodist Churches in Scotland were to be admitted – superintendents, circuits and all – to the Church of Scotland, was rejected by the Methodist congregations in 1979.

In 1977 the Multilateral Conversation produced a short statement on the need for the unity of the Church to be visible. A united ministry to serve a united Church should lead on to a Plan of Union. The Assembly referred this to presbyteries for comment. The replies from presbyteries displayed a wide variety of views. Only six accepted the statement without critical comment. There was widespread insistence on diversity as something to be safeguarded. In commenting on the replies in its 1978 report, the Inter-Church Relations Committee under the convenership of Professor James Whyte stressed the value of diversity as 'having its ground in the inexhaustible riches of the mystery of Christ, the differences of culture and historical situation being but the prism that breaks up the rays of light'. Denominations could be seen as instruments whereby, in the providence of God, aspects of the diversity of the Gospel have been preserved. The Committee noted that the fear was widespread, and not altogether unreasonable, that schemes of organic unity would tend towards uniformity. The Committee favoured further exploration of the concept of 'reconciled diversity' as an immediate aim. In 1979, under a new convener, the Inter-Church Relations Committee was at pains to stress that 'reconciled diversity' could never be a final goal, and the Committee recommended a radical re-assessment of diversities for the purpose of achieving reconciliation and a new unity. One is left with the impression that the regard for the value of diversity was being replaced by something rather different.

A report from the Multilateral Conversation was submitted to the 1985 Assembly. Although the two predominant branches of the Church in Scotland – the Church of Scotland and the Roman Catholic Church – were never likely to unite, the report was prefaced by the usual fervent prayers that the Church should achieve organic unity. It then proceeded to propose 'a form of personal ministry not just at the congregational level but also at the regional level' and referred to permanent moderators of presbyteries, superintendents and so on. What it did not explain was that neither the Church of England nor the Episcopal Church in Scotland would be prepared to enter into full communion with any church in which ministers were not ordained within the historic episcopate. Stripped of the trappings the simple fact emerges that the Anglican acceptance of the validity of Church of Scotland orders remains the kernel of the problem. Communion with the episcopal churches will be secured only at the expense of an admission, however tactfully disguised, that the Church of Scotland, since the Revolution Settlement of 1690, has not been a true church. We have not advanced an inch since the Assembly's refusal to accept this proposition in 1933.

Following the receipt of replies from presbyteries, the General Assembly of 1986 accepted a proposal from the Board of World Mission and Unity that the Board should request the Multilateral Conversation to note the widespread rejection of any concept of a threefold order of ministry and of episcopacy as a distinct order.

It is an interesting indication of the extent to which ecumenism had, in some quarters, eroded the traditional Scottish attachment to the presbyterian system that in 1978 the Committee of Forty, appointed to examine the organisation of the Church, could express this tepid view on presbyterianism:

It may still be true that the presbyterian form of church government is an appropriate one for Scotland in the latter half of the twentieth century; but if it is – and some have always taken leave to question it – it will be so on the practical basis that in that way Christian people in Scotland can best find freedom to express the faith that is in them through evangelism, mission and service to all their neighbours.

Even more surprising was the indifference of the Committee of Forty to the rights of the members of the congregation to choose their minister. Emphasis was placed on the duty of the presbytery to give more substantial 'assistance' than hitherto. The proposal that a vacancy committee should be required to consider a list of names put to it by the presbytery received a frosty reception in the Church at large and the balance was restored by the approval in 1983 of proposals made by an Assembly committee over which Dr Andrew Herron presided.

To many of us, the essence of being Scottish lies in the Church of Scotland – Calvinist in cast of mind and presbyterian in government. The ecumenists would strip the Church of Scotland of these characteristics but profess to preserve something they call Scotland. The Church and Nation Committee in its 1982 report discussed 'the Scottish identity'. It dwelt on the geographical and economic reasons for the separateness of Scotland and made little reference to our Calvinist and presbyterian roots, except at one point to hint a fault in our presbyterian system. Egalitarianism was said to spring from a deeply-felt attitude and obviously the Committee averted its eyes from the attitude of its predecessors to Irish Roman Catholic immigration (described later) when it said 'an associated characteristic is our openness to immigrants of other sects, creeds, races and colour'. The Church was defined as the body of Christians in the community and for the future it did not go beyond a vague hope for 'a renewal of Christian worship and commitment'.

When the Abbé Sieyès joined the French Directory in 1799, he was asked how he had fared in the Terror and replied that he had survived. Perhaps no more can be said of presbyterianism in relation to the attacks made on it in the name of ecumenism. Yet that is not the whole story. The strength of presbyterianism in the minds and hearts of the members of the Church of Scotland has been shown by their steadfast adherence to the faith of their fathers against a sustained attack by prominent churchmen who have managed to control the main committees. Some statistics are of interest.

The Report of the Department of Home Mission to the 1983 General Assembly drew attention to the fact that in 1980 recorded church membership, as a percentage of the adult population, was 13 per cent in England, 23 per cent in Wales, 37 per cent in Scotland and 80 per cent in Northern Ireland. Whereas only five per cent in England belonged to the Church of England, 25.8 per cent in Scotland belonged to the Church of Scotland and other presbyterian churches. As the Report commented:

> From these figures, it becomes apparent that, whatever changes may presently affect the Church throughout the land, the Scottish position still remains distinctive in terms of denominational loyalty. By and large it would still be true to say that Scotland is Presbyterian in a way in which no other part of the UK exhibits so clear a denominational loyalty.

From all of which it is fair to conclude that Scotland is still staunchly presbyterian at heart and in fact. However kindly the Scot may be disposed to those who favour some other form of church government, he wishes to be left in peace to practise a form of government which is acceptable to him and which he believes to be agreeable to the Word of God.

Notes and references to Chapter I

1 Knight, W A (1871). *Colloquia Peripatetica*. Hamilton, p9.
2 Beveridge, Henry (trs) (1844). *Calvin's Tracts Relating to the Reformation*. Calvin Translation Society, Vol I, p34.
3 Cowan, Ian B (1976). *The Scottish Covenanters 1660-88*. Victor Gollancz, pp146-47.
4 Macaulay, Lord (1900). *Miscellaneous Writings and Speeches*. Longman Green, p706.
5 In recent years the General Assembly of the Church of Scotland has acquiesced in a similar form of representation of the Church of Scotland for periodic informal discussions with the Church of England General Synod. The Church of England has a larger 'lay' element in their team than the Church of Scotland.
6 *Manchester Guardian*, 14 December 1957.
7 Joint Report (1957). *Relations between Anglican and Presbyterian Churches*. SPCK.

II

The Ecumenical Movement

Fifty years ago, if it had been felt in the Church of Scotland that its Christian effectiveness should be improved in some respect, the General Assembly or a presbytery would have plunged straight into the detail of how it was to be done. Today we are expected to consider everything in the context of the ecumenical movement, the supporters of which judge any proposal on evangelism, doctrine, worship or organisation in the light of the contribution it will make to the institutional unity of the Christian Church. Indeed, it has on occasion been proposed that we should do nothing to improve our system of presbyterian government till we have called in other denominations and secured their agreement. Future generations will be amazed at the strength of the ecumenical movement among the ministries of the churches and puzzled by the uncritical acceptance of its tenets in so many quarters.

The main support of the ecumenical movement lies, not in the membership of the various denominations, but in a section of their ordained ministries. Reformed churches are being urged to unite with churches in which the clergy have an entrenched domination. Even where the laity are admitted to the process of government in these churches, it is on terms that leave the clergy with a veto, as in the separate houses of the Church of England Synod. One effect is an endeavour to increase the power of the ordained ministry in Reformed Churches. The movement spends endless time discussing the nature of the ordained ministry and it gives rise to statements such as that 'the distinctive mark of the Church is the ministry of Word and sacrament'. The effort to foist episcopacy on presbyterian churches is but one facet of a general tendency to exalt the ministry in a way that is inconsistent with the fundamentals of presbyterianism and, some would say, with the spirit of the Church Gospel.

The ordinary member of the Church of Scotland needs to take stock where the ecumenical movement is leading him. There are pressure groups dedicated to the institutional unity of the Church. There are elderly ministers in whose minds slogans about 'the sins of our divisions' have become so engrained that they are incapable of fresh thought on the subject. A re-appraisal is needed by fresh minds concerned solely with the furtherance of Christ's Kingdom and willing to be guided by the lessons of the history of the ecumenical movement and by the prognosis for its future.

Common ground

Christians of all denominations recognise that there is unity in the Church. In the Reformed tradition, the visible Church is catholic or universal and, under the headship of Christ, consists of all of those throughout the world who profess the Christian faith. Each branch or denomination has its own conception of faithfulness to the Gospels and judges other churches by the extent to which these other churches are pure by its standards. None of the particular branches is perfect. In the past, often in periods of strong faith, there has been rivalry and even hostility between denominations and more particularly between their leaders, but no Protestant has doubted that there is a universal church which embraces them all, however fragmented by differences in doctrine and organisation. This is clearly stated in the *Scots Confession of 1560*.

The ecumenical movement aims at turning this unity into an institutional amalgamation. Because of this desire to secure an institutional amalgamation, the ecumenists always undervalue the unity that already exists. Archbishop Fisher, who wanted to have inter-communion but who accepted the continued existence of separate churches, put this forcibly when he wrote:

> Ecumenists will not really know what they are talking about unless they keep ever in mind that the Universal Church is always in a state of organic union with Christ, without which it could not exist.

Reasons for ecumenism

The vision of an institutional organic unity of all professing Christians has a strong emotional appeal. It was felt by the reformers of the 16th century, as it is felt today. The difficulty is that existing denominations do not fit into the vision, since they are a mass of rigid opinions, doctrinaire stands and entrenched prejudices. There is a vast gulf in thought-processes between the well-meaning individual who longs for unity in a vague and nebulous way and the ecclesiastical politician who invents elaborate and ambiguous formulas to try to reconcile the churches as they are.

Professor George Yule's pamphlet on *Mission and Unity in Christ* was published in 1986 by the Handsel Press, with a commendation by the convener of the Board of World Mission and Unity. Professor Yule pleads for an institutional unity beyond inter-communion and beyond friendly co-operation between churches. He agrees that some of the issues which divide Christians, like the primacy of the papacy, episcopacy, women priests, the mode of Christ's presence in the eucharist, the nature of the inspiration of the Bible and the nature of our justification 'are matters of deep concern and must be taken seriously'. However, he argues that the central truth of the Gospel, that God has accepted us unconditionally in Jesus Christ, makes all other issues secondary. He urges that institutional unity should be constructed round the belief in the love of God, Father, Son and Holy Spirit, as displayed in the death and resurrection of Christ.

Professor Yule fails to rebut in a convincing way the arguments that the churches already have spiritual unity and that the main aim should be to ensure that what the convener in his foreword calls 'deadly rivalry' is replaced by friendly co-operation and joint enterprises. Professor Yule does not at any point explain what form the institutional unity which he seeks is to take. Is any existing church prepared to accept that the substance of the faith is adequately expressed in his formulation? Those who deplore 'the sins of our divisions' and propose to eliminate them have a duty to explain what structure of doctrine and government they propose. It is not sufficient to express general sentiments, however sincerely held.

Undoubtedly a factor in the growth of ecumenism has been the extent to which Biblical criticism has been interpreted as undermining the authority of the Scriptures. If the New Testament is treated as the product of the early churches, rather than as the direct revelation of God's will, then one searches for a worldwide organisation which can interpret the Christian message in modern terms. But the more one examines this proposition the less it seems true to Christ's teaching.

It is not without significance that the growth of the ecumenical movement has coincided with the progressive decline in the hold of Christianity on the mind and heart of Western man. It is argued that there is a waste of resources through the duplication of services by different denominations. However, to represent the movement as akin to the amalgamation of units which takes place in a declining industry would be unfair. The ecumenists are moved by a vision, however impracticable that vision may be. The danger is that, in an unsympathetic climate of opinion in the public at large, the ecumenists will find it more congenial to discuss theological niceties in little conclaves of like-minded clerics than to preach Christ's gospel to the world at large.

A record of failure

The ecumenists present themselves as having something new and fresh to tell the world, as interpreters of Christ's teaching in a present-day setting. In fact, we have now had many years' experience of their work and should be able to draw lessons from that experience.

In matters of doctrine and organisation, the history of ecumenism is largely a history of failure – a failure which ecumenists put down to the entrenched conservatism of denominations. In fact, the real reasons lie elsewhere.

The mergers which produced the present Church of Scotland are not really relevant in this connection. These were unions between churches of the same original stock, with the same form of church government and all subscribing to the *Westminster Confession of Faith*. Ecumenism is primarily concerned with efforts to merge churches with different statements of belief and different structures.

History

Towards the end of the last century, there were plans, notably among churches in the United States, for a loose federal unity between denominations. The eventual outcome was the establishment in 1908 of the Federal Council of Churches. Each denomination would preserve its own identity but all would work together and establish a common ground in their beliefs. A church union on these lines was in fact effected in China in the

1920s: and the idea of federation has had its supporters in Western countries throughout the years. Thus the Inter-Church Relations Committee, in its analysis in 1959 of the replies of presbyteries on the Bishops Report, said that some presbyteries took the view that the aim should be 'a federation of Churches, differing in policy but bound together by practical collaboration, good brotherly relations and fully reciprocal inter-communion'. Again, those in the United Reformed Church who in 1981 opposed union with the Church of England under the covenanting proposals favoured 'a form of federation in which we create patterns of committed co-operation with clearer links between the churches'.

For better or for worse, this approach has been consistently and strongly resisted, being replaced by an attempt to secure organic unity. This has involved efforts to compromise on some issues and acceptance of the inflexible views of some denominations on other issues. While the creators of an ecclesiastical organisation put together by a series of ingenious, if often ambiguous, formulas might regard their work as a wonderful intellectual exercise, it would make no real appeal to the hearts of men. It is not surprising that attempts to compromise on different traditions rarely succeed.

The ecumenical movement has led to the preparation of many statements of belief. For the most part, they deserve the description given in a rather unlikely place – *The Economist* of 14 July 1973:

> Compromises on economic and political matters are quantifiable: the interests concerned can be sliced, measured, portioned out. Compromises on religious truths, which are the currency of the churches, cannot. They are not material for settlement by a vote in committee. It is not easy to see how in the interests of unity a quart of Real Presence could be traded against two pints of Anglican orders. But a Christian superchurch would require such super-bargains.
>
> Of course, a clever theologian, like a clever Parliamentary counsel, is perfectly capable of finding forms of words which can satisfy two or more sides. But articles of religious belief should express a fully believed truth, or they are nothing. A judicious selection of bland phrases designed to smooth out differences of interpretation might actually make sizeable groups of believers leave their churches. And there is more to religion than its intellectual content. There are such things as styles of worship, forms

of ministry, traditions of private piety. There are differences in emphasis on moral matters. An attempt to satisfy a maximum number of people from different traditions could alienate many of them. The looser the formulation the greater the danger that people will simply walk out through the holes.

In Communist countries, where Christianity is an evangelical force, there is no sign of any desire to escape from the dogmas of materialism into general-purpose Christianity. They want something more full-blooded, and they join the Baptists or Jehovah's Witnesses. Organisations that seek to further the ecumenical cause offer little spiritual food and tend to concentrate on economic and political problems. Christians then find themselves operating in fields where other agencies are better equipped to do what is required. Our Founder taught what individuals should believe and how they should behave and offered no political platform.

One of the cankers at the root of the ecumenical tree is that it favours the intolerant. If one group makes no claim beyond saying that presbyterianism is agreeable to the word of God and another group says that episcopacy is an essential feature of the Church, it is the presbyterian who goes to the wall. It is nonsense to say that the super-church would incorporate all the best features of its constituent parts. The great virtues of the presbyterian system could not survive in an episcopalian setting.

The New Testament does not prescribe a single pattern of ministry and there was a variety of forms of ministry in the early church: but this has not deterred the episcopal churches from making their claims that a church must have the threefold pattern of bishop, presbyter and deacon. The American Episcopal Church took the lead in enunciating, as a basis for church union, what became known later as the Lambeth Quadrilateral. One controversial element in what was described as the 'sacred deposit' which was 'essential to the restoration of unity among the divided branches of Christendom' was:

> The Historical Episcopate, locally adapted in the methods of its administration to the varying needs of the nations and peoples called of God into the unity of his Church.

The advantage to the Anglican communion of this statement of the road to unity was that it need make little or no changes of substance in its own standards and organisation. It saw itself as the *via media*, which others should join. This was set out, with disarming candour, by Dr Patrick Rodger, then Bishop of Oxford, in a debate on ecumenism in the Church of England Synod on 4 July 1985. The late Professor Ian Henderson, of the Chair of Systematic Theology in the University of Glasgow, in *Power without Glory* (1967), brought out with great clarity the extent to which the ecumenical movement was taken over by the Anglican churches, notably the American Episcopal Church and by elements in other churches (including the Church of Scotland) which were attracted to Anglican ways. If Professor Henderson were alive today, he would find support for his point of view in the report, published in February 1985 by the Church of England Board for Mission and Unity, on the World Council of Churches' statement on church unity entitled *Baptism, Eucharist and Ministry* (the Lima document). The Board said:

> 'Baptism, Eucharist and Ministry' and The Final Report (of the Anglican-Roman Catholic International Commission) are not simply the text of a few theologians who were members of the two commissions. The Church of England, through its General Synod, diocesan and deanery synods, has already influenced the form and content of the texts. We have had a hand in shaping them.

Methodist Church

The recent history of Methodism is full of lessons for the student of the ecumenical movement. Ecumenism involves compromise and compromise usually results in a situation that satisfies noone.

All branches of Methodism accepted the doctrines of the Christian faith, as set out in the historic creeds but insisted that the heart of Christianity lay in the personal dealings of the individual with his Creator.

In doctrine, however, there was a split between those, like John Wesley, who were of an Arminian cast of mind and believed that all might be saved and those who accepted Calvinism (and in particular predestination). This led to the formation of the Calvinist Methodist Church of Wales (now the Presbyterian Church of Wales) and of Lady Huntingdon's Connection. There were differences about the duties of ministers and lay people in matters such as the placing of ministers in charges and the administration of the sacraments. There was dissatisfaction with the failure to evangelise sufficiently vigorously. This led to the formation of Primitive Methodists, Bible Christians, Free Methodists and the New Connection.

The Bible Christians, Free Methodists and New Connection merged to form the United Methodist Church in 1907. The Wesleyan Methodist Church, the United Methodist Church and the Primitive Methodist Church merged into the Methodist Church in 1932. The whole process and results were set out by Mr Robert Currie in *Methodism Divided*, published in 1968.

Both unions involved compromises on deeply held convictions relating to the balance between ministers and lay members. The result was to give greater authority to ministers than some of the smaller churches had permitted. This is a feature of all ecumenical ventures, because the advocates of unity come largely from the clergy. The Wesleyan Methodists gave much greater power to ministers. Thus only ministers could station ministers in congregations. The other Methodists asserted lay rights to share in stationing ministers, as in other decisions. The Methodist Church, created in 1932, admitted laymen to the stationing process, but limited them to advising the ministers and vetoing their decisions. This has not proved to be a satisfactory position.

During the 25 years of the separate existence of the United Methodist Church (from 1907 to 1932), it had a lower rate of growth than the Primitive Methodists and the Wesleyan Methodists had had.

The establishment of the Methodist Church in 1932 was preceded by statements that 'with the consummation of union a great forward movement on quite unprecedented lines is anticipated: is indeed inevitable'. Nothing like that happened. The Methodist Church's membership decreased by 140 000 (17.7%) between 1932 and 1964. This was a difficult time for most churches, but it could not be said that ecumenism had promoted mission.

An attempt in 1957 to stage celebrations on the 25th anniversary of the 1932 uinion was still-born. There was not enough to celebrate.

In spite of this experience, the Methodist ecumenists could still, in 1962, see a union of the Church of England and Methodism as producing 'a great new Church, far better and greater than either Church in its separation, into which have come the full treasures, in thought, worship, prayer and order, of each; and have there been reconciled and mutually enlarged.'[1] This is mere wishful thinking. There are occasions when the triumph of hope over experience is inexcusable.

Methodist experience is that the smaller constituent denominations of a united church lose heavily. If chapels are closed down, it is usually theirs that are chosen for closure. They have to accept other forms of worship and the majority group tends to elect church leaders from its own numbers, though at the outset after the various unions an effort was made to avoid this. Many Methodists have felt that the united church has a remote and cumbersome bureaucracy. None of this supports the claims of the ecumenists that there can be variety in unity and that each tradition makes its special contribution to the united church. Equally the claim that the rationalisation of resources would promote evangelisation has received no support from the experience of the Methodist Church – such rationalisation as has occurred has been accompanied by severe losses in membership.

Anglican/Methodist Negotiations

The Lambeth Confererence of 1920 set out the conditions under which the Anglican communion was prepared to join with other churches, but little progress had been made before the Second World War.

After that War, it is usual to record as a landmark the Cambridge sermon of Archbishop Fisher on 3 November 1946 in which he urged the Free Churches in England 'to take episcopacy into their systems', as a means of working towards full communion with the Church of England. What is often overlooked is that the Archbishop was not contemplating 'the fearful complexities and upheaval of a constitutional union' and indeed he said in the same sermon that there were tensions within the Church of England that had to be resolved before there could be any question of constitutional affiliation with other denominations. Wise and prophetic words.

However, the Methodist Church in 1953 decided to enter into discussions with the Church of England provided that the Church of England acknowledged that the present discussions were within the Christian Body (that is, that Methodism was a church), that the Methodist Church had the same liberty of interpretation as in the Church of England about the nature of episcopacy and of the priesthood and that the Methodist Church would be free to preserve inter-communion and fellowship with other non-episcopal churches. The Church of England in 1955 agreed that any discussions were taking place 'within the Body of Christ', but that 'matters of Anglican essential order and discipline would need to be safeguarded' as would 'the office and function of a priest in the Church of God'. These conditions, vague though they were, contained the elements of future trouble. The scheme which was eventually worked out provided for an interim goal, described as 'stage one', when the Methodists would have bishops and 'stage two', perhaps 20 years later, when there would be a full union. The problem, in the services of reconciliation, was how to bring Methodism within the historic episcopate without throwing doubt on the validity of the Methodist ministry. The Methodist Conference accepted the scheme by a 79.4 per cent majority in 1970. Eventually in 1972, the scheme failed to secure the necessary 75 per cent majority among the clergy and laity in the Church of England General Synod. The scheme illustrated many of the problems presented by these ecumenical ventures – a good deal of hostility, a great deal of apathy and a complete lack of enthusiasm at the local level in both churches, the unpredictability of the result because of disagreements and tensions within both churches, and the refusal of the Anglo-Catholic wing of the Church of England to go an inch towards admitting the validity of non-episcopal orders.

Nothing is more poignant or more illustrative of the dehabilitating effects of ecumenical negotiations than the words in which Mr J M Turner concluded his account of the scheme, in which he referred to Methodist leaders as 'mesmerised by union'.[2]

> The writer published an article a few days after the Synod's vote which called on Methodism to recover its pioneering use of manpower and buildings, to come to terms with the rebirth of the theology of experience in the charismatic movement, to find modern ways of presenting Wesley's doctrine of Christian perfection, to renew worship so that it can be a vehicle of evangelism as well as nurture. Methodism must recover, albeit in modern ways and modern terms, its passion for evangelism. Above all it must play its proper role in the great dissent of our time – a nonconformity against all that degrades people. 'World population, world poverty, pollution, the continued threat of thermo-nuclear war

are the big issues.' Clearly some of this agenda was taken up in a 'recovery of nerve' in the 1970s but there arose also ominous signs of fragmentation and a growth of irrationalism which was not predictable in the 'secular sixties'. The truth of the matter could well be that Methodism was simply not strong enough for an independent mission.

United Reformed Church

The Presbyterian Church of England and most congregations in the Congregational Union united in 1972. The architects of the union claimed that it marked a great step forward and that the enthusiasm which it would engender would result in a great missionary surge. In fact the membership of the United Reformed Church (URC) is falling more quickly than that of any other major denomination. There have been compromises on beliefs and practices in the forward march to greater church unity, represented by the union of the URC with the Churches of Christ. One result is that ministers of the URC are no longer automatically accepted for charges in the Church of Scotland. Many presbyterians within the URC must be disillusioned and wish that the URC had never been cobbled together.

Covenant for Unity

Those who seek institutional unity develop an absorbing interest in the intellectual problems that are raised and it is not, therefore, surprising that by 1973 elements in the Methodist and the United Reformed Churches were making a further effort at English church unity. This resulted in the Ten Propositions (1975) which were accepted, subject to various reservations, by the Church of England. Finally there was the Covenant for Unity, described in an inter-church report issued in 1980. In the long run all were to accept episcopacy 'in the historic succession' but for an interim period ministers exercising episcopal functions (eg seven-year moderators of presbyteries in the United Reformed Church) were to be allowed. There was to be mutual recognition as complete Christian communities, with a mandate to work together towards organic unity. It was ominous for the success of the Covenant scheme, and for all future schemes purporting to make progress by accepting ministers exercising episcopal functions without being ordained by bishops in the historic succession, that three influential representatives of the Church of

England refused to sign the report. This minority said that even a temporary dispensation in favour of a few non-episcopally ordained ministers who exercised quasi-episcopal functions involved a departure from a fundamental principle of Catholic order and would be a further barrier to closer association with other parts of the Church Catholic.

The proposals in the report, having been accepted (amid a lot of disagreement in the United Reformed Church) by majorities in the other churches in 1982, failed to get the necessary two-thirds majority among the clerical members of the Church of England General Synod.[3] Archbishop Runcie's commendation of the Covenant was so full of qualifications that one bishop announced that the Archbishop's speech had persuaded him to vote against the Covenant. The Churches' Council for Covenanting was dissolved and Dr John Habgood (now Archbishop of York), writing in *The Times*, said that the Synod's decision had brought to a halt a process which started with the Lambeth Conference of 1920 and that there was no escape from the bleakness of the immediate ecumenical outlook.

Although the Church of Scotland Inter-Church Relations Committee in its 1983 Report to the General Assembly claimed that one of the Committee's main concerns was to keep the Church in touch with inter-church developments elsewhere, it made only the briefest passing reference to the failure of the Covenant proposal in England and did not explain in any way its significance in relation to the Committee's activities. Some Assembly reports should be headed 'This is propaganda. For the full facts you must go elsewhere'.

Ecumenism and Presbyterianism
The great majority of the members of the Church of Scotland wish to preserve the presbyterian system of church government. Even if that majority were to be eroded, experience in other parts of the world shows that a union with churches of different traditions would split the Church of Scotland in two. Substantial numbers would remain true to the faith of their forefathers. Ecumenism would be obtained at a heavy price. One cannot but wish that the ecumenists showed more respect and affection for the Church of Scotland as we have known it and a better appreciation of the likely consequences of their proposals.

The United Church of Canada was formed in 1925 of method-

ists, congregationalists and presbyterians. While 3728 presbyterian congregations went into the United Church, 784 (including some of the largest) did not. There was therefore a tragic
separation of presbyterian from presbyterian. The smaller
Presbyterian Church which resulted is the third largest Protestant church in Canada with over 165 000 members in 8 synods
and 44 presbyteries. In 1977, a similar union of methodists,
congregationalists and presbyterians took place in Australia.
Again a substantial minority of the Presbyterian Church of Australia refused to join the uniting church, mainly because of dissatisfaction with the doctrinal position of the new church. In both
Canada and Australia, about one third of the members of the
presbyterian church remained separate. These were unions between non-episcopal churches. How much more intense would
be the feeling in Scotland against the type of union contemplated
in *Christian Unity – Now is the Time.*

Scottish Aspects

The vast majority of the Protestants in Scotland are members of
the Church of Scotland. The only other church of any size is the
Roman Catholic Church.

There is no foreseeable prospect of organic union between the
Church of Scotland and the Roman Catholic Church. In 1977,
the General Assembly approved a report of the Panel on Doctrine on the points of agreement and disagreement with the
Church of Rome which *inter alia* said:

> Because the Church of Scotland recognises the existence of a
> variety of particular churches, none of which is uniquely perfect
> and complete, it does not necessarily hold that there must be or is
> ever likely to be one single universal and organically united
> Church, nor does it accept that among all the churches at present
> any particular one represents the norm from which all others have
> diverged. It does believe that the present state of division ob-
> scures the true nature of the Church, and that reunion is to be
> aimed for where it is possible that that nature may be more clearly
> manifested; but this involves change and transformation on all
> sides, for all are imperfect.
>
> This difference in approach is not seen by the Church of Scot-
> land as a reason for holding back from contact and co-operation
> with the Roman Catholic Church. It is, however, a factor which
> needs to be clearly understood on both sides. In particular, the
> Church of Scotland welcomes the new openness and brotherli-

ness shown in the last generation by the Roman Catholic Church, and wishes to reciprocate them. It accepts that, just as central elements in the present Roman Catholic position are unacceptable to it, so too the Church of Scotland standpoint is one with which Roman Catholics have difficulty in agreeing. It therefore offers and asks for mutual understanding of the serious difference that still exists in this area.

One is, therefore, entitled to ask what purpose is served by modifying the present doctrines and government of the Church of Scotland in the interests of an organic unity of Christians in Scotland which will never be achieved in the foreseeable future? There has been no suggestion that hymns should be gradually phased out and stricter adherence to *The Westminster Confession* required in order to move towards union with the Free Church. Why should there be pressure to adopt the episcopalian form of government and to exalt the sacraments at the expense of the preaching of the Word, if the only result would be some form of marriage with the small Scottish Episcopal Church? This is advanced under the ecumenical banner, but in the Scottish context this is somewhat spurious. One is driven to the conclusion, which the late Professor Ian Henderson reached many years ago, that many of the professed ecumenists are simply enamoured with Anglican ways. In the past, the leaders of the Church of Scotland were content to exercise a leadership based on their personal qualities. The intellectual superiority of the average Scottish minister over the average Anglican clergyman has been admitted even south of the border.[4] It is sad if some of our present leaders feel that they need the trappings of episcopacy to be able to assert themselves and if some ministers feel that they would be more at home with weekly communions than with the preaching of the Word. Sadder still when those responsible for producing our orders for worship enshrine this as the norm.

But there is more to it than that. The Episcopal Church is heavily involved in the negotiations which the present Archbishop of Canterbury has described as being designed to lead to a union between the Church of Rome and the Anglican communion by the year 2000. This target is most unlikely to be met – probably it will never be met because of the instinctive dislike of Rome by the English people and a dislike of the 'liberal' and wayward views of some Anglican bishops by the Roman Catholic

Church. But does the Church of Scotland really want to be beguiled down this path, even part of the way?

Meantime, in terms of public worship, the aim is to produce an Anglican type of service – emphasis on the sacraments rather than the Word, involving weekly communion as the central feature of the Sunday morning service. Inevitably preaching suffers, if the communion is what matters and the sermon takes second place. Those who think along these lines should study what is happening in the Church of England. Dr Leslie Francis, a church sociologist, has made a study of trends in the English countryside.[5] Of course, there are exceptions but his general picture is of tiny aging congregations. *The Times* religious affairs correspondent summed up the position as 'The Church of England faces extinction in the countryside in the next 20 years'. If that is happening in England, the effect of replacing the Scottish type of service, with its emphasis on the preaching of the Word, by an alien Anglican form of worship would be truly catastrophic.

The Church of Scotland should consider where it is going in ecumenical matters. In spite of a long record of failure, the ecumenists assume that time is on their side. They tend to treat Assembly decisions against them as temporary aberrations which can be reversed at some later date. Successive Assemblies have encouraged this state of mind by hedging their bets – rejecting proposals or referring them to presbyteries for them to reject, but continuing in existence the inter-church discussions which lead to further similar proposals. Meantime, where they have control of Assembly committees, the ecumenists put forward proposals on doctrine, worship and church organisation which are intended to further the cause of institutional unity.

The goal of the Church as one institution is unattainable on two grounds. First, there is a cleavage on fundamental issues between Roman Catholicism and Protestantism which cannot be bridged in any foreseeable future. Second, any universal church put together by ingenious formulas, would fracture under pressure from the growing number who see Christianity as involving a simple faith and a rudimentary organisation. After all, the resurgence of Islam has occurred without any elaborate organisational changes.

Unsubstantiated claims

Professor James Whyte has referred to the unsubstantiated claims made by the ecumenists. It is not clear whether these claims – made against all the evidence – are the result of mental inertia or of a belief that, if repeated often enough, they will become true or at least will be accepted as true.

The Mind of Christ

The ecumenical movement is entitled to take John 17:21 as its favourite text. What it is not entitled to do is to represent the prayer that Christian believers all may be one as a divine instruction for institutional unity. The text obviously deals with matters of the spirit and we often work together in greater harmony if we are in our separate branches, than if we are engaged in what amounts to a power struggle within a gigantic organisation.

If Christ had wished to construct a monolithic church, he would have outlined the necessary structure in his teaching. The hierarchical church to which the ecumenical movement seems to be committed tends to produce leaders surrounded with pomp and display which seem strangely out of keeping with New Testament teaching. Likewise in matters of doctrine, if uniformity had been intended, it is surprising that the New Testament contains so many crucial passages on which different interpretations can legitimately be entertained. Nor does Christ's teaching, as revealed to us, correspond at all with the practice of the ecumenists. If they had existed in Palestine at the beginning of our era, they would have busied themselves trying to reconcile the Sadducees and the Pharisees. They would have spent much time and energy trying to devise a formula on life after death which was acceptable to the Sadducees who did not believe in the resurrection of the body and to the Pharisees who did. Do you see Christ as a formula creator? To him, the good was the enemy of the best. The Pharisee, who had many admirable qualities, was condemned because he did not attain to the ideals which Jesus depicted.

If Christ returned tomorrow, would he be impressed by the sight of church leaders sitting in cosy parlours discussing fine points of theology in the interests of ecumenism, or would he tell them to get out and preach the gospel to the world at large?

Perhaps, however, the ecumenists would not wish to push too hard their claim to be giving effect to Christ's commands. It was contended that the *Bishops Report* of 1957 represented the work of the Holy Spirit, but, when the Church of Scotland rejected the report and later proposals of the same sort, no ecumenist felt obliged to leave a church which had rejected God's will as revealed to the authors of the Report.

Effect on Evangelism

In favour of greater institutional unity, it is constantly said that it would cause a great surge of evangelical fervour and that the churchless millions will not listen till the church is one. There is no reason to believe that either proposition is true.

The claim that institutional amalgamations generate spiritual fervour in the membership gets no support from the experience of such ecumenical unions of churches as have taken place. Quite the reverse.

John Highet in *The Scottish Churches* (1960) analysed the evidence for the proposition that the divisions keep the unchurched away and found it unconvincing. He added:

> For the non-churchman to invoke the division of Christendom as the reason for his standing apart has always struck me as a rationalisation – a particularly attractive one, too, for it induces in the user a sense of ethical uplift and superficially sounds convincing and indicative of lofty standards, for which no doubt he hopes his listener will give him due credit. 'Then why not come in and help the churches to work for unity?' is the riposte this rationalisation deserves but does not always receive.

One would more readily accept the idea of the potential believer kept out of the fold because of our divisions if one knew of someone desperately anxious to have a car but unwilling to buy one until they devise one standard make!

Mr J M Turner in *Conflict and Reconciliation* (1985) points out that, although it is an ecumenical commonplace that the world will not accept Christianity while the Churches are divided, little sociological evidence is ever furnished in support of this statement.

The Livingston Ecumenical Experiment has not led to a great upsurge in membership, and the Presbytery of West Lothian has expressed its disappointment in the total number of Church members in Livingston.

A more realistic approach is to accept that the process of unification, so far from providing a stimulus, will raise many practical difficulties and cause much friction. The moral is that no one should embark on church union if there are widespread and serious differences of opinion within a denomination or if the general impulse towards union is weak. Those were the conclusions drawn by the contributors to *A History of the Ecumenical Movement, 1517–1948* and nothing that has happened since has shown them to be wrong.

There is a particular Scottish aspect to this problem, arising out of the form that ecumenism has taken. It has a strong slant towards the adoption of Anglican ways: and the Anglican Church has not been conspicuously successful as a vehicle for extending Christ's kingdom.

The Church of England has roughly 1 800 000 members. The population of England over 20 years of age is about 33 000 000. Therefore between five and six per cent of the population are members of the Church of England. The Church of Scotland, with rather more than 850 000 members, has about 23 per cent of the adult population of 3 700 000. An ardent presbyterian would argue that, if England had given effect to the Solemn League and Covenant and become presbyterian, the present membership would (on the Scottish analogy) be 8 000 000 not 1 800 000.

The Episcopal Church in Scotland has never numbered more than 50 000: and Anglicans who come to live in Scotland often prefer to join the Church of Scotland.

Yet we have Church of Scotland committees that spend their time trying to get us to adopt Anglican ways. They exalt the sacraments at the expense of preaching the Word and they infiltrate Anglican ways of worship. Is it surprising that numbers are falling?

Would all best features be preserved?
One of the favourite arguments of the ecumenists is that a united body can bring together and exemplify all the best features of the uniting churches. This has not, however, been generally accepted. In 1946, Dr John White drew attention to the difficulty of devising any practical scheme of organic union between a church holding the historic episcopate and a church holding the historic presbyterate, *without greatly impoverishing the spiritual treasury of both*. He desired church unity 'but not at the sacrifice of the traditions and rich spiritual heritage of our Church of Scotland'. He was forced to conclude that, unless by some miracle, there

should be a change of attitude among Anglicans, the Church of Scotland by 'taking episcopacy into its system' would have to turn its back on its historic past and avert its eyes from the monuments it had set up to the martyrs it revered.[6]

Experience supports John White's views. If much of the strength of presbyterianism flows from the parity of presbyters, this is in no way preserved if a hierarchical form of government is introduced.

Episcopacy and presbyterianism are incompatible. As has been said 'Nowhere does the spirit of independence and jealous safeguarding of rights and liberties burn so strongly as in the average Scottish presbytery'. Episcopacy on the other hand requires submission to the bishop and dependence on him. If you introduce bishops into the Scottish Church, either the unhappy bishops would sink under a mixture of silent contempt and open rebellion or their position and authority would have by degrees to be strengthened and safeguarded in all the courts of the church and the loss of the presbyterian virtues would be complete.

It is also argued that any united Church would display great variety in beliefs and worship. The report of the Anglican-Reformed International Commission 1984 says that the Church is and always will be characterised by great diversity. This seems to refer to national and cultural differences, but even at the local level it is contemplated that churches would 'express both the unity to which God calls his whole creation in Christ and the diversity which properly characterises the human family as God intends it to be'.

One has to face the fact that parties within churches usually tend to be intolerant of the views of other parties. If you think that your views are right, you push them, particularly within your own denomination. Widespread apathy encourages this intolerance among those with inflexible views. A hundred illustrations spring to mind.

Take the *Book of Common Order*, published in 1979 by the Committee on Public Worship and Aids to Devotion. The Church of Scotland has for generations celebrated the Lord's Supper once, twice or four times a year: and that has been the wish of the great majority of its members. Nevertheless, the committee decided that it would arrange the book on the basis that the Lord's Supper was celebrated at every morning service.

Regardless of the views of most church members, the committee decided that experience of the Holy Spirit is 'richest where worship is ordered according to the eucharistic pattern'. The normal Church of Scotland service is relegated to page 42 where it appears as an apologetic appendix described as 'Morning Service where Holy Communion is not celebrated'. We have reason to be thankful that the National Church Association took upon itself to prepare and publish a *Reformed Book of Common Order* which accorded more closely with traditional Church of Scotland practice. But, if tolerance and variety are virtues, why did not the Committee on Public Worship and Aids to Devotion include in their book the form of communion service published in the *Reformed Book of Common Order*?

The lack of interest in variety could be illustrated from some reports put before the Assembly. They are drafted to boost one point of view. Inconvenient developments are ignored or played down. Questionnaires are loaded. There is often an absence of objectivity, to an extent which would be unacceptable in documents prepared in secular activities, which set out issues for decision.

The same intolerance can of course be illustrated from the experience of other churches. Over a long period of years, the Anglo-Catholic wing of the Church of England has been single-minded in pushing its views, regardless of the wishes of large sections of the Church of England. Nothing is more poignant, in Archbishop Garbett's *Claims of the Church of England* (1947) than his description of ritualistic and other changes made in Church of England churches against the wishes of the parishioners which caused great bitterness and led many to leave their parish church, never to return to it again.

In April 1987 the Bishop of Chichester (Dr E W Kemp) wrote a letter to *The Times* defending the choice of Church of England bishops by the Prime Minister, as a way of ensuring that the episcopate fairly represented the main groupings in the Church. He said that it was part of the vocation of the Church of England to show that the tradition of Catholic, Protestant and liberal theology can be held together in one communion. 'History seems to me to show that ... there is need for the Crown and Parliament to hold the ring and prevent any one of the groups in the Church from making changes which undermines the existence of the others and destroy that vocation.' If church groups may behave like this in the Church of England, which prides itself on its comprehensiveness, what is one to expect in churches where compromise is less highly regarded?

Are divisions purely historical?
The ecumenists are fond of arguing that many of the divisions are purely historical and that it is, for example, iniquitous to perpetuate them outside Europe where they have little relevance. The Churches in North India and South India are quoted as examples of what should happen elsewhere. In fact, many of the divisions are being perpetuated outside Europe, because they still reflect differences in the interpretation of the Gospels and in the application of the Gospels to local situations. The report of the Anglican-Reformed International Commission 1984 (*God's Reign and Our Unity*) admits:

> Plans for organic union between Anglican and Reformed churches which at one time seemed very promising have collapsed in Nigeria, Ghana, Sri Lanka, the Sudan, Canada, Australia and New Zealand. The United States Consultation on Church Union (COCU) has been at work for more than twenty years and has been obliged to move from the search for full organic union to exploring the idea of a covenant as a first stage, but progress towards this intermediate goal is uncertain. Proposals for covenanting in England and New Zealand have failed and those in South Africa have suffered a serious setback.

Stumbling blocks
Denominational Divisions
Within many churches there is considerable diversity of view on fundamental points of doctrine. This results in links being formed that cross the denominational boundaries, and this is to be welcomed. Evangelicals in the Church of Scotland have been heard to say that they feel in closer rapport with members of the evangelical wing of the Church of England than with some other members of the Church of Scotland. But this diversity of view within denominations is a serious obstacle to organic unity. With which party within the church are you negotiating? You may have negotiated with those in sympathy with your views, only to find that those who are at the other end of the spectrum wish to defeat the proposals for unity that had been laboriously put together. This bothered Archbishop Lang in his day.

Percipient minds have seen this problem for a long time. It is a pity that more attention was not paid to their views. Before the First World War, leaders of the Orthodox Church were pointing out that there could be no real union between their communion and the Anglican Church until the ambiguity of Anglican doctrinal formulas and the wide variety of interpretations which were permitted were resolved and the Anglican Church itself became more homogeneous. Archbishop Fisher said to Dr John White and others that the Church of England was in no condition to amalgamate with any other church.

Problems with Anglicans
The insistence by important elements in the Anglican communion that bishops in the historic succession are an essential feature of a true Church is an enormous stumbling block in the way of ecumenical progress. There is no sign of any weakening on this score in the Church of England and the Scottish Episcopal Church. The Anglo-Catholics are adamant and Protestant elements are not prepared to risk the Church of England being split in two on the issue.

Compromise proposals brought forward in other churches with a view to luring their members along the road are fundamentally dishonest, since the promoters know that the ultimate goal of full communion with Anglicans will not be achieved unless there are bishops in the historic succession who have a special responsibility to maintain and further the unity of the church, to uphold its discipline and to safeguard its faith.

Moreover, it means the open or tacit acceptance that the uniting church has not been a real church and it also means the creation of a barrier against non-episcopal churches with which it has had close relations in the past. No self-respecting church can accept these terms.

Woolliness in Thought
Faced with a world that is increasingly difficult to understand, the ordinary man looks to the church for certainty and a measure of clarity. The ecumenists offer him complicated formulas, devised – not to meet his needs – but to reconcile conflicting denominational views.

There is nothing new in this. Calvin was present at the conferences organised by the Emperor at Worms and Ratisbon in

1540 and 1541. There he became ashamed of the attempts to arrive at a compromise by Melanchthon and Bucer:

> Philip (Melanchthon) and Bucer have drawn up ambiguous and insincere formulas on transubstantiation to see if they could please our opponents without themselves surrendering anything. I do not agree with this scheme .... They do not fear equivocation in matters of conscience, than which nothing can possibly be more harmful.

The cause of true Christian unity is better served by warm co-operation between branches that frankly recognise that, on certain fundamentals, they interpret the Gospels and the traditions of the Church differently.

A Roman Catholic author, writing in *The Times*, 30 June 1984, drew attention to the unwillingness of ecumenists to speak of religious truth.

> The horrid fact is that if you make a religious statement that actually means something, you imply that somebody else may possibly be wrong; and that would not do at all. It would be divisive and unecumenical, a breach of the proprieties. The practical answer is obvious: confine yourself to social altruism, sentimentalised up with a little Christian terminology. If you venture beyond that, be careful to say nothing that excludes its contrary: go in for platitudinous waffle, high-sounding but vague. That is how many of us do proceed, with paralysing consequences for religious literature.

Woolliness in Language

Ecumenists have developed a very wordy form of writing about matters of doctrine and government which may seem to reconcile widely different theological views but which does not yield a living, vibrant faith, for which men and women would be prepared to die.

Their literature abounds in somewhat incoherent statements such as that 'the goal of church unity is the reconciliation of humanity and the whole universe to God' and more specific but unsubstantiated affirmations such as that 'denominational divisions are both contrary to the will of God and moreover call in question the Church's mission to the world'. Every pamphlet or report on church unity is prefaced with woolly incantations of this sort.

One technique is to approach every subject from a number of points of view. This involves a great deal of repetition, but it enables widely divergent opinions to be encompassed within the treatment: 'A' is referred to paragraph 'X' where his opinion is set out and 'B' is referred to paragraph 'Y' where, in a different treatment of the same subject, his opinion is given due weight. The result is a mass of ambiguities and vagueness. The same result is also achieved by avoiding English words that have a fairly precise meaning and using instead the transliteration of Greek or Aramaic words with no precise English equivalent so that the meaning becomes unclear. All this can be seen in *Baptism, Eucharist and Ministry*. And it infects a great deal of other writings, as in the statements by the Panel on Doctrine on *Baptism* (1983) and the *Ministry* (1985).

Tillich, the German theologian, spoke of the need for church leaders to get outside the 'theological circle' and discuss matters with the man in the pew. Today we must break through the ecumenical circle and deal realistically with the problems of the churches.

The ultimate goal
The World Council of Churches has made various efforts to express the goal at which the ecumenical movement is aimed. The constitution of the Council now provides for the goal of visible unity in one faith and in one eucharistic fellowship expressed in worship and in common life in Christ. What this means in practical terms remains somewhat nebulous. The New Delhi Assembly of 1961 envisaged a foundation of local unity; but on what matters there would be uniformity and on what matters diversity was not clear. The Nairobi Assembly of 1975 referred to the united church as a conciliar fellowship of local churches which are themselves truly united: and the Lima statement of 1982 tried to lay the foundations for the problems of organisation that arise.

As more and more reports are prepared of ecumenical discussions between denominations, the question remains to be answered – what, in practical terms as distinct from mere rhetoric, is the ultimate goal? The Anglican-Reformed International Commission (1984) says: 'We still struggle to understand and express the form which unity should take.'

Archbishop Fisher had assumed that churches would remain separate and would not, as an immediate objective, go beyond being in full communion with each other. This was to be achieved primarily by the Reformed Churched 'taking episcopacy into their system'. This idea of independent churches in communion with each other is still a strand in ecumenical thinking. It represented the first stage in the schemes discussed between the Church of England and the English Free Churches. Discussions between the Church of England and Lutheran Churches have also taken this form.

A greater favourite is, however, a series of national churches in full communion with each other. The ecumenical movement flinches when face to face with nationalism. A few brave spirits have asked why the ecumenists want national churches, but the truth is that the ecumenists think that the denominations can be flattened but not nationalism. Anglicans who aim at national churches assume that a united Church in Sweden would be almost wholly Lutheran in its received tradition, the Anglican element would be strong in Uganda, the Roman Catholic in South America and so on. Our Church of Scotland ecumenists are much more pusillanimous. If nationalism is to be accepted, why should not the other churches in Scotland accept that the Church of Scotland has provided a church agreeable to the mass of its people and accept presbyterianism for the united church which they strive to achieve? Principal Rainy made this point as long ago as 1896.

It might be thought that the Orthodox Churches would be attracted to the idea of national churches in full communion with each other, but in fact the Orthodox Churches remain firmly of the opinion that they alone represent the true Church.

The Roman Catholic Church, with its centralised administration, would contemplate only a limited amount of national diversity and would never contemplate a series of independent national churches, whatever the links between them. It would demand one universal liturgy and one universal canon law.

The truth is that the goal of unity tends to be seen by each communion in terms of its own history and ideas. In spite of all their talk and endless discussions and reports, the Churches are no nearer any real agreement about what they are trying to do: and there is no consistency in ultimate objectives in the various separate discussions that are being conducted between groups of churches.

Step by Step

Faced with uncertainty about the ultimate goal, the ecumenists are agreed upon a step-by-step approach to unity. This has the advantage that ecumenists start with the easy issues and can claim success at that stage, and proceed, often in a time span of many years, to the difficult issues where grave differences exist. The disadvantage of this approach is that vast amounts of time and labour can be wasted, and have in fact been wasted. In many cases it would be better to start with the difficult issues – if no real progress can be made then this would be brought to notice at an early stage.

Another disadvantage of the step-by-step approach is that the practical goal remains obscure. 'We still struggle to understand and express the form which unity should take.' But the goal is important. If the Church must be one, then Protestant Churches must combine with the Roman Catholic Church: and Rome shows no tendency to compromise on what it regards as fundamentals.

Do we think that a vast monolithic church, with a hierarchical organisation headed by a Pope or a Council, is a practical or desirable goal in any future that can be foreseen? The answer must be an emphatic 'No'. As the Panel on Doctrine pointed out in 1977, in a report now largely reproduced in *Agreement and Disagreement* by Dr Alasdair Heron,[7] the differences in doctrine and government are too great to be bridged. In any event, if the Church of Scotland ceased to adhere to the Scottish Reformation, it would cease under its own constitution to be the Church of Scotland. If amalgamation with, or absorption in, the Roman Catholic Church is out of the question, then the prospect is of at least two churches and all the talk about the Church being one loses force. If two, why not three or four or five? On the step-by-step approach, churches will make compromises and weaken their effective witness to try to attain an ultimate unity which is out of their reach. The report of the Multilateral Conversations (1985) speaks of 'a vision of a united Scottish Church which will be a fuller expression – fuller than our Churches can be in separation – of the one holy, catholic and apostolic Church in our land', but if there is no reasonable prospect of one church in Scotland this is empty rhetoric. It is not clear why an amalgamation of the Church of Scotland with some relatively small churches greatly improves the present position, especially if the price to be paid is a high one and if, as is certain, a substantial number in the Church of Scotland would never accept episcopacy and would form a separate body, claiming to be the true Church of Scotland.

Religious movements try to create a climate of opinion in which opposition to their tenets is regarded as antediluvian or just perverse. There is nothing new in this. The Revd Septimus Harding in Anthony Trollope's *Barchester Towers* lamented that a man is condemned if it can be shown that he does not belong to some new school of thought established within the previous score of years. Ecumenism runs true to form. In the *Dictionary of National Biography*, it is recorded that Sir Donald MacAlister, Principal of Glasgow University from 1907 to 1929, was a staunch presbyterian. Presumably today it would be said, as a defect, that he was somewhat lacking in the ecumenical spirit. We must not be over-impressed by the claims made on behalf of a movement which, in the form which it has taken, is almost certainly a passing phenomenon in the long march of history.

The ecumenical conference held at Swanwick in September 1987 represented an effort to put some life into the dying cause of ecumenism. The British Council of Churches is to be dissolved, and the Roman Catholic Church has agreed to participate fully in the new body that will be set up in its place. It seems to be assumed that the new organisation will be used to endeavour to secure a common stance on public issues, and this has led to criticism that on some important matters the result will be bland, ambiguous and ineffective statements which paper over differences between the churches. The procedure is in any event not suited to the Church of Scotland which can speak authoritatively only through its General Assembly and which would not authorise individuals to negotiate any point of view to which it had not itself subscribed.

But the main object of the new machinery will be to work towards institutional unity. The statement issued at the end of the conference ignores the fact that the churches already have spiritual unity and says in effect that unity can be secured only in one Church, united in faith, communion, pastoral care and mission. The unity sought is said to be not uniformity but 'legitimate diversity', though no indication is given as to who will say what is legitimate and what is illegitimate. As always in ecumenical discussions, the form of the eventual united church is left completely vague. What is contemplated is a step-by-step approach to a goal which in fact will never be reached and which would be disastrous for the cause of Christ if it were reached. What is now essential for the Church of Scotland is that its members insist that discussion at this stage concentrate on the nature of the eventual goal. It cannot be doubted that presbyterianism would represent an 'illegitimate' diversity. How narrow would be the scope for diversity was indicated obliquely by Cardinal Hume when he said that there was already considerable diversity within the Roman Catholic Church. We need a list of requirements on which the Roman Catholic Church and the Anglo-Catholic element in the Church of England could be expected to insist. Members of the Church of Scotland must then ask themselves whether they wish to engage in a long process of compromising principles and making reluctant concessions when the end (if ever reached) would be the destruction of so much that the Church of Scotland has stood for in the past and still believes to be both important and relevant today. The ecumenists must not be allowed to keep the ordinary member in ignorance of what they are prepared to concede at the end of the day. Institutional unity and the necessary degree of diversity are in practice quite incompatible. The unity of the Holy Catholic Church is spiritual and not institutional. The task of evangelisation is urgent and the Church of Christ should engage in it on a number of fronts and in a variety of forms.

Conclusion

What are the reasons for the overall failure of the ecumenical movement? Why has the movement, in the form which it has chosen to take, failed in the past and lost any appeal that it ever had to the majority of church members?

One reason is obvious. The vision of one visible church of all believers, which has a great attraction to most Christians, is practicable only in a world where a few simple truths of the Christian faith are held to be basic. It would be a world which allowed diversity of doctrine and laid down few rules, if any rules at all, about organisation. Hinduism shows that such a faith can exist and live. A few fundamental concepts have provided an enduring thread through the long history of Hinduism. A Christian Church which valued unity above all else would show the greatest diversity in doctrine, organisation and worship, and would allow full recognition to all.

Much latitude would seem to have been desired by many of those who took part in what was called the Inter-Church Process, in which members of various denominations met in the spring of 1986 for prayer, reflection and debate. They were not necessarily typical members of their churches and might have been expected to support the ecumenical movement. There seems to have been a realisation that organic unity was not practicable in the foreseeable future, and there were references to inter-communion and some form of federation. The unity they sought was not the form of unity which the ecumenists would produce. 'There was a clear recognition that, in matters of worship in particular, people are individuals with differing needs and tastes. Much freedom and variety is therefore both necessary and desirable adequately to meet these needs. Diversity, it was felt, is good'.

Ecumenism fails because the constituent parts of the Christian Church show no inclination to accept this pattern. The Roman Catholic Church regards as fundamental and essential to salvation the acceptance of tenets that have no scriptural warrant. The episcopal churches have long abandoned the more tolerant views of their 17th century forebears and insist on the historic episcopate as an essential feature of a church. Churches which adopt a truly Christian tolerance find that the only road to unity lies in accepting tenets that they do not hold or in accepting ambiguously expressed compromises that endeavour to conceal the true state of affairs. Throughout the churches there is a desire for co-operation and joint working – this cannot truthfully be represented as a desire for institutional unity.

The ecumenical movement is working against two forces that are running strongly and deeply as the twentieth century moves towards its close. One is the need to recognise that Christianity takes many forms and can meet all essential needs only if its diversity is allowed to develop. The other is the need to involve the ordinary members of every church more deeply in its affairs. The ecumenical movement runs counter to the real needs of the times. It busies itself with long-standing differences between churches, and shows little interest in modern developments and modern needs.

Many-sidedness of Christianity

The glory of Christianity, and the source of its strength when it has been strongest, has lain in the many facets it presents. The Scriptures reflect this diversity and admit of a variety of interpretation on many points. North America, South America, Africa, Asia and Australia are developing those aspects of our faith that meet their special needs. This will develop further as the years go on and nothing will stop it. Moreover within each country there is a broad division between those who adhere to the authoritarian tradition and those who are evangelical in outlook. The more that hierarchical systems and bureaucratic machinery are developed, the greater will be the determination of the evangelicals to cut away from it all and to seek a simpler form of the faith.

If there is a great resurge of loyalty to Christ (and we must believe and pray that this will happen soon), there will almost certainly be a desire to break free from institutional fetters. The House Church Movement is a complicated affair but it contains elements that accord with this view. An elaborate organisation that has been patched together will just fall apart or seem irrelevant.

The ecumenists recognise that there is a continuing demand for diversity and they purport to see the need for it. But they give no clear indication how they are to meet it and in fact they cannot meet it. They refer vaguely to variations in worship but they have views on doctrine which determine their views on worship. Having thrashed out formulas on doctrine and agreed upon a form of government, acceptance will surely be required of members of the united church. That is the point of endless discussions, the expenditure of much thought and effort and the abandonment by some of cherished views, if at the end of the day members of the new church are told that adherence to these agreed tenets is optional? Some diversity is possible with old confessions of faith, where there is a let-out in matters that do not enter into the substance of the faith; but here we are dealing with newly forged instruments. Moreover many of the leaders are not tolerant of views other than their own. They place a high value on institutional unity and they will not be prepared to see any fragile structure they have put together put in jeopardy by those who do not share their views.

The only way for Christians to carry out their evangelical task is in separate churches, parts of the Universal Church, consisting of members who subscribe to certain interpretations of the Scriptures. The report of the Multilateral Conversation infers that separate churches must be enemies. Nothing is further from the truth. In fact it is often easier to be on close terms with someone in another church than with someone in one's own denomination with whom one does not see eye to eye, especially if parties in a church are struggling for control.

Ordinary Members

It is universally agreed that the clamant need of the present day is the full engagement of the members of a church in all its activities. The ecumenists have perforce to recognise this and they refer to the ministry of the whole church and the need for every member to exercise a form of ministry. But all this tends to be words, signifying little, because the ecumenists are in practice engaged in exalting the ordained ministry and creating a hierarchy of authority within the ordained ministry. Authority comes from bishops within the historic episcopacy and some of this is delegated to the lower grades in the three-fold ministry of bishop, priest and deacon. Episcopacy may have had its uses at some periods of history, but, as education spreads, a church should not need a hierarchy and it is doubtful whether, with episcopacy, the membership of a church can realise its potentialities as the Body of Christ.

A presbyterian church, on the other hand, is uniquely placed to make a reality of the ministry of the whole church. There is the place of the elder in all the courts of the church and greater responsibility can be placed in the hands of the ordinary members of the church without impairing the system of government.

It is high time for presbyterians to awake and proclaim that in their form of church government they have a unique contribution to offer to a democratically-orientated 20th century.

Notes and references to Chapter II

1 Davies, Rupert (1962). *Methodists and Unity*. Mowbray, p96.
2 Turner, John Munsey (1985). *Conflict and Reconciliation*. Epworth Press, p214.
3 In matters of importance, the General Synod can determine that a higher percentage than 50 per cent is required in voting by

bishops, clergy and laity. In the case of the Anglican/Methodist scheme, the percentage had been 75 per cent.

4 *Cf* Matthews, W R (1969). *Memories and Meaning*. Hodder & Stoughton, p116.
5 Francis, Leslie J (1985). *Rural Anglicanism*. Collins.
6 Muir, Augustus (1958). *John White*. Hodder & Stoughton, p422.
7 Heron, Alasdair I C (1984). *Agreement and Disagreement*. Handsel Press.

III

Statement of the Faith

If we turn aside from misguided efforts at rigid institutional unity and aim instead at friendliness and collaboration with other branches of the Christian Church, we shall be like Christian in *Pilgrim's Progress* when he was freed of his grievous load and we shall go forward 'glad and lightsome'. We can apply our minds to the problem of how to improve the Church of Scotland in accord with the mind of Christ as revealed in the Scriptures. We can go forward in full collaboration with other branches of the Church in Scotland and elsewhere. There is now fortunately the friendliest co-operation between the various denominations at all levels, and everything should be done to foster this. We need no admonition from the participants in Multilateral Conversation to 'abjure the enemy syndrome'. The sense of a common task is widespread throughout the Christian community.

If, with God's help, we can find it, there is a key which would open the door to a rejuvenation of the Church of Scotland. It is worth searching for. The Kirk has in the past been a Scot's most precious possession, which he treasured at home and which he took to all quarters of the globe, if he left his native land. The basis of that affection for the Kirk was the belief that it provided a sound organisation for the faithful propagation of Christ's teaching, as revealed in the New Testament.

Need for a Statement of the Faith

The Church of England Archbishops' Commission on Christian Doctrine that reported to the Church of England in 1938 contained a sentence of profound truth:

> Nothing can be discovered by man about God apart from the revelation of himself by God to man; *nor can anything be effectively revealed by God to man apart from an activity of human reason in apprehending it.*

On what constitutes the Christian faith and on the relative importance of different aspects of the faith, the Scriptures, on some important matters, can be interpreted in different ways. If a body of believers are to have a coherent and firm faith, they cannot escape from the need to say where they stand in these matters. The malaise that affects the churches today is not so much due to defects of organisation as to the absence of a clear conception of the faith.

Some limits must also be accepted on the pursuit, within the Church, of theological issues as an intellectual exercise. It is not easy to reconcile 'Jesus Christ, the same yesterday, today and forever' with the habits of some theologians who, like the Athenians described in the Acts, spend their time in nothing else but telling some new thing. If the Divinity Faculties of some Scottish universities are to examine religious beliefs in a clinical fashion, divinity students should go with a clear understanding of the faith against which they can test what they hear.

Some who oppose the preparation of a statement of belief argue that it is an attempt to devise a test by which the orthodoxy of church members would be examined. In these days when tolerance is ranked higher than orthodoxy, they argue that this represents an effort to revive heresy hunts. This is not the reason for wanting a statement of the faith. A coherent statement of belief would help the Church to retain its members and enlist new ones. The ordinary member of the Church, and for that matter the ordinary member of the General Assembly, is in a state of puzzlement where the Church stands on some major issues.

There is no question of a confession of faith being regarded as superior to the Scriptures. 'The function of a Confession is not to bind but to loose: it should help us to understand and not provide a substitute for understanding: it should be a means and never an end.' (G D Henderson: *The Burning Bush*.)

A Confession of Faith is needed:

(a) to bring together the teaching of the Scriptures on fundamental problems

(b) to deal with theological problems, affecting the organisation of the church and other questions, on which the teaching of the Scriptures has to be interpreted.

A Confession of Faith has to deal with our idea of God and with the nature of the Church and of authority within the

Church. If we were a loosely organised religion, like Islam or Buddhism, it might be possible to leave members with the Scriptures and regard that as enough. For better or for worse, Christianity is the most highly organised form of religion that the world has seen: and a church must have views on the nature of the Church, on the questions where authority lies and on the nature of the sacraments.

It is sometimes overlooked that one of the main purposes of *The Westminster Confession* was to enable the ordinary member to know where his church stood on fundamental issues. It was a sense of this need that apparently led to demands for a fresh look at it. There are certainly enough strange ideas about for a member of the Church of Scotland to feel bewildered.

There are two aspects of the matter. First, a member expects his church to have clear and specific views on important spiritual issues. Second, he expects to have them set out in a way he understands. It would be a mistake to imagine that the Scottish cast of mind is content to leave these issues in a state of uncertainty, under which some theologian is called on to expound what he regards as the views of the Church. Religion is too serious a matter to be left to academic theologians. John Ruskin may have done some foolish things; but he also said some wise ones, one of which was that a religion which the common man cannot understand is not worth having.

A Presbyterian church has an especial need for a statement of the faith. We need a faith and an organisation which the ordinary member can understand, practise and defend. Presbyterianism can be described in terms of the parity of ministers and of the parity of ministers and elders and these are essential features; but the real driving force behind an on-going presbyterian church is the sense of 'belonging' that it can inspire among the members of the church. Jesus Christ alone can invigorate the members of the church, and His Gospel must be at the centre of all activities; but, in so far as the work falls within the church, every endeavour must be made to involve members in all aspects of the church's work – the exposition of the Gospels, the formulation of doctrine, the work of the church and its government. The great advance in general education since the early days of the Reformation is itself a ground for greater general involvement in the affairs of the church. If the ordinary member can be fully engaged, then, as Principal Rainy put it, from the broad base of the believing people the sap rises through the ascending courts of the church. We shall never draw adequately on the general body of members for the recruitment of ministers and church workers unless there is diffused throughout the people substantial knowledge of all the issues that concern the church.

There should be a broad band of views that represents the general mind of the church. A national church has to accommodate a fairly broad spectrum of views, but on main issues there should be agreement where the church as a whole stands and what will be the basis of its teaching. That does not mean that there should be a heresy hunt against those who hold minority views unless the matter enters into the substance of the faith. But the holder of a minority view on fundamental issues should be expected to apply the majority view where positive action is required. Thus on the eldership there have been, and no doubt will continue to be, differences of opinion about its nature; but the church needs a view which expresses general opinions and which is propounded as such.

There is a further reason for a statement of the faith. The authority exercised by the courts of the church is one of the essentials of presbyterianism. Doctrine is not the province of any individual or group within a hierarchical system, but is the concern of the whole Church, acting in and through its courts. A member of the Church may find himself, as minister or elder, called upon to form a view on questions of doctrine and as a member of the Assembly to take a decision. A Confession of Faith is needed, as a framework within which discussion takes place. Put another way, a presbyterian church, to be effective, needs a confession of faith, as something corresponding to the written constitution of a secular state. Otherwise the General Assembly could be adrift without a compass to guide its course. Without doubt, it was a realisation of this truth that led the General Assembly in 1974 and presbyteries in 1984 to refuse to abandon *The Westminister Confession* in the absence of any acceptable substitute. Equally, the tendency to make greater use of the Barrier Act procedure and to refer Assembly business to the presbyteries for their views owes something to a realisation that the Assembly lacks an adequate modern framework of belief within which to operate.

And the same reasoning applies to the other courts of the church – synods, presbyteries and kirk sessions. They need an authoritative guide in deciding the issues that come before them.

There is yet another ground for having an accepted statement of the faith which arises out of the special circumstances of the Church of Scotland. Article I of the Articles which formed the basis of the 1929 Union sets out the beliefs that are essential for the continued identity of the Church. It is difficult to see how adherence is to be shown, including continued adherence to the Scottish Reformation, if not in a statement of the faith.

Form of a Statement of the Faith

There are broadly three ways of presenting the Church's beliefs. One can:

(a) rely on the ancient creeds and have arrangements for interpreting the Church's position on later issues or

(b) have a statement of what are described as the Church's beliefs and accept that individual members will vary in their acceptance of these beliefs or

(c) have a statement of belief to which members are expected to subscribe.

Each method has its advantages and disadvantages.

Ancient Creeds

The Lambeth Quadrilateral, which is the basis of Anglican ecumenical policy, described the Nicene Creed as a sufficient statement of the Christian faith: and, as indicated below, the panel on Doctrine was attracted to this in various proposals that it put before the Assembly. The Panel has clearly been imbued throughout with the belief that the cause of ecumenism would best be served by carrying as little denominational impedimenta as possible. A short statement is difficult to conceive as adequate, unless there is an authoritative body which can interpret the Church's position on fundamental current issues. Presumably the Bench of Bishops endeavours to fulfil this function in an episcopalian church. Would the Panel on Doctrine meet the need in the Church of Scotland?

Whether we should have a Panel on Doctrine at all is doubtful. The late Dr George Dryburgh, to whose efforts at the time of the Bishops Report the Church owes so much, considered that the Panel should never have been set up and that the Church should appoint *ad hoc* committees to deal with specific theological issues. Formally, the Panel accepts that it does not issue authoritative statements on doctrine and that it is a consultative and co-ordinating body dealing with remits from the General Assembly and its committees. There is, however, always a danger that the Panel takes itself too seriously. The statement in one of the Panel's reports in 1972 that 'the Panel does not claim that it alone has the responsibility of expressing what the Church believes' may have been intended to disarm criticism, but is in fact somewhat alarming. In any event the Church has indicated plainly enough that it is not prepared to accept adherence to the ancient Creeds as sufficient.

Beliefs Attributed to the Church

An alternative is to express the faith in terms of what the Church believes. This is sometimes represented as allowing gradations of commitment to individuals, while retaining the essential standard of faith for the whole community. This has been elaborated by an Anglican clergyman, the Rt Revd Richard Holloway, now Bishop of Edinburgh, in *New Vision of Glory* (1974). He summarises the matter as follows:

> The individual's personal apprehension of the faith may be meagre and hesitant, fraught with private doubt and the limitations of his own historical situation. Nevertheless, it is still possible for him to confess the total faith of the community because it is the community's and because he wishes to identify himself with the community, if only by intention.

The Declaratory Articles, setting out the constitution of the Church of Scotland in spiritual matters and accepted by Parliament in 1921 as 'lawful' refer to various beliefs held by the Church of Scotland. The aim was not, however, to provide a statement of belief but to facilitate union with the United Free Church. The Panel's efforts to use the First Article as a statement of the substance of the faith foundered on its unsuitability for this purpose.

In 1986 the House of Bishops of the Church of England Synod issued a statement entitled 'The Nature of Christian Belief' which was intended to allay the disquiet felt as a result of the widely publicised views of Dr David Jenkins, Bishop of Durham. In dealing with the Resurrection, the bishops' statement said *inter alia* that 'as regards belief that Christ's tomb was empty on the first Easter Day, we acknowledge and uphold this as expressing the faith of the Church of England.' At a press conference to launch the statement, the religious affairs correspondent of *The Times* asked the bishops present whether they personally believed what was attributed to the Church of England. None of them said 'yes' or 'no' and they gave involved answers. The habit of attributing views to the Church but not subscribing to them does great harm. If the trumpet gives an uncertain sound, who shall prepare himself to the battle?

The Panel's ill-fated statement for popular use was in the form of a statement of beliefs attributed to the Church. This is not what is needed at present. The world craves for personal anchors in religion. There is a danger that a statement of the Church's belief loses credibility, as members reiterate the qualifications on their acceptance of its tenets. Moreover emphasis on what the Church believes seems to be at variance with the Protestant ethic.

Confessional Statement

Any statement of the faith should set out the truth as we see it, as individuals and as a Church.

In various respects we live in a time of turmoil when there is no consensus on the substance of the faith. The degree of agreement on fundamentals that existed in past centuries is often overstated, but the field of disagreement on fundamentals has undoubtedly expanded.

Nevertheless there are enough unsound ideas floating about for it to be desirable to set out the faith as the great majority of the members of the Church of Scotland see it.

In 1935, the General Assembly approved a Short Statement of the Church's Faith which was described as 'an outline of the main articles of Christian belief suitable for the instruction of learners and for the help and guidance of believers'. It was commendably clear and unambiguous (unlike the wordiness of some recent statements) but, viewed as an authoritative statement of faith, it failed to enter into subjects in sufficient depth. It was not intended that it should do so.

Various modern confessions of faith, adopted by Reformed Churches, exist. The Presbyterian Church of England devised one not long before its union with the Congregationalists. The North American Presbyterian Churches have devised modern confessions. I have set out in the Appendix a statement of belief, based on the statement prepared by the Presbyterian Church of England, and incorporating parts of *The Westminster Confession* and of the *1935 Church of Scotland Short Statement*. It is, however, difficult to secure detailed acceptance of the terms of any statement and as a consequence difficult to give it authority. The confession drawn up by the Presbyterian Church of England contained many excellent passages but it gathered little authority around it before the union with the Congregationalists put an end to its brief life. No one refused to join the United Reformed Church because the new confession was being discarded.

Is a new Confession of Faith attainable?
In 1968, The General Assembly asked the Panel on Doctrine to consider the place of *The Westminster Confession* as a subordinate standard and the reference to the Confession in the preamble and questions used at the ordination of ministers and elders.

In its report to the 1969 Assembly, the Panel proposed that *The Westminster Confession* should lose its position as the principal subordinate standard and indeed that there should be no subordinate standards. The Confession, with the ancient creeds and the *Scots Confession of 1560*, were to be regarded as historic statements of faith. It was proposed that there should be a short statement of fundamental doctrines to which ministers and elders would have to subscribe on ordination. Although the proposals secured general approval from 49 out of 63 presbyteries, they were rejected by the 1974 Assembly. The ground of the Assembly's rejection was that, until a new statement of belief received general acceptance, the Panel's proposals left the doctrinal position too uncertain. There was wide agreement that *The Westminster Confession* should be retained until the Church had accepted another confession.

Meantime a different approach was being made to the subject. A special committee on the doctrine of the Church had reported in 1969 and secured an Assembly decision that the Panel on Doctrine should prepare a single statement of belief for popular use. The Panel took up this task after the Assembly decision on its other proposals in 1974.

The concentration on a statement of belief 'for popular use' was open to objection. There should be one statement of belief,

to which all can subscribe. That is the Scottish tradition. Whatever their shortcomings, *The Westminster Confession of Faith* and
the Longer and Shorter Catechisms grappled with difficult problems and did not burke them. For example, a young child was
expected to learn, and later to understand, the answer to the
question 'What is effectual calling?'. A document should speak
up, not down, to the church member.

The statement as it eventually emerged was not really a statement of belief. It was to some extent a chronological account of
scriptural events, with comments that tended, on some important issues, to be agnostic in tone.

Publications like *Priestland's Progress* and the great interest
aroused by the late Bishop John Robinson's books are reminders
that one should not underestimate the extent to which theological issues can engage the mind of the ordinary church member.
Nor should one underrate his intelligence as compared with the
professionals.

The opening words of the statement 'The Church believes in
God' are unfortunate and indeed offensive. One is reminded of
Carlyle's comment on the woman who said that she accepted the
universe – 'By Gad, she'd better'. There is indeed a failure to
stress adequately the greatness and majesty of God and his absolute goodness. Emphasis on these attributes is necessary because of the tendency in some quarters to portray God as a big,
loving Daddy with easy moral standards.

The statement makes no reference to the Virgin Birth and this
made it desirable that the authors should explain how they interpret the incarnation, that is, how they relate Christ's divinity to
his humanity. Books like the Hansons' *Reasonable Belief* (1980)
set out the various alternatives as they appear to the modern
mind. The statement seems to infer different views at different
points. And the same is true of the crucifixion and resurrection.
The problem with which Paul wrestled, how man with all his
defects could ever reach communion with God, does not seem to
be at the centre of the Panel's thinking. No Christian can regard
a statement of belief as adequate that does not spell out the meaning for us of Christ's cross. It is not enough to say vaguely 'In
Jesus Christ, God has dealt effectively with all our estrangement,
homelessness and frustration, with evil, sin and death' or again
that the disciples had been 'reconciled to God through the life,
death and resurrection of their master'. The point is important.

Paul made little reference to Jesus's teaching. He concentrated on the meaning of his death and resurrection.

About the resurrection, as about Christ's birth, life and death, the statement says that 'we today find it no easy task to separate the facts from the traditions which the facts inspired'. The only fact mentioned is that for the disciples Jesus became the risen Christ, altogether one with God the Creator – a somewhat inadequate statement. What are the authors of the statement saying or inferring about the empty tomb?

The statement, without addition or qualification, that God has 'given us a foretaste of what he has in store for the whole creation' is presumably meant to deny our Calvinist heritage and perhaps to hint at universalism. Yet there are few who believe that Hitler or Stalin will end up in heaven and it seems to be difficult to reconcile such views with some of Christ's sayings.

It is simply not true that *the* distinctive mark of the Church is the ministry of word and sacrament. The statement fails to explain why elders predominate in kirk sessions and have an equal say on all questions in the higher courts of the Church.

The preaching of the Word should come before the administration of the sacraments, as it did in the *1935 Short Statement*. The statement describes the Church in section five but, apart from a brief reference to the proclamation of the Gospel, it does not give any prominence to the reading and preaching of the Word. This is playing down the missionary role of the Church. A report before the 1977 Assembly pointed out that the preaching of the Word is addressed to all, whereas the sacrament is restricted to those already in some branch of the Church. To say, in relation to the sacraments that 'sometimes actions speak more loudly than words' is in effect to denigrate the appeal of Christianity to the mind. The present sad state of the Church of England is a reminder of what happens if preaching withers and too much emphasis is placed on the sacraments.

The Church needs some anchors in dealing with the faith. The statement failed to provide enough. Scots need some link with *The Westminster Confession of Faith*, which is in our bones. This provided no link.

I have dwelt on the imperfections of the statement – now dead and buried – at some length because it is the nearest that the Panel has so far come to setting out a modern confession of faith.

The statement was described as based on material provided by committees drawn from the four University Faculties of Divinity and from presbyteries, and then worked over by the Panel. As suggested by the Panel, the General Assembly sent the statement to presbyteries for comment. Apart from indicating that some presbyteries had objected to the omission of any reference to the Virgin Birth, the Panel did not give any account of the points raised by presbyteries. The Panel concluded that the statement did not commend itself to the Church as a whole and that the comments by presbyteries gave no indication of the lines upon which a revision could profitably be attempted. The whole episode shows how difficult it would be, in the Church of Scotland at this juncture, to get a satisfactory new statement of belief.

The 1978 Assembly agreed to drop the draft statement of belief for popular use and asked the Panel on Doctrine 'to consider the status of *The Westminster Confession of Faith* as the Church's subordinate standard and to report to a future General Assembly with, if so advised, new proposals the definition of the Church's doctrinal standards'.

The Panel reported in 1984, after lengthy consultations. The Panel retained the concept of a subordinate standard, though it had said in 1969 that the need for this was widely doubted. It proposed, however, to remove *The Westminster Confession* from its pre-eminence by having four subordinate standards – The Apostles' Creed, the Nicene Creed, *The Scots Confession of 1560* and *The Westminster Confession*. This could also be said to be reducing the current, as distinct from the historic, significance of a subordinate standard, in so far as there were differences between *The Scots Confession* and *The Westminster Confession*. The Apostles' Creed and the Nicene Creed are covered by *The Westminster Confession*. The Panel also proposed – contrary to doubts it had expressed in 1969 – to use the First Article, as embodying the substance of the faith, in ordination. These proposals were rejected by a majority of presbyteries (27 to 21). The 1985 Blue Book deals with the rejection in a perfunctory way. The reasons for rejection were undoubtedly a feeling that the First Article was not suitable as a summary of the substance of the faith and that the object of resurrecting *The Scots Confession* was not clear and the subject of suspicion. Conservatives and modernists both saw objection in what was proposed, though on different grounds.

The Westminster Confession is described in the Declaratory

Articles as containing the sum and substance of the faith of the Reformed Church. The churches that eventually reunited as the Church of Scotland had, however, used the concept of 'the substance of the faith' to cover essential parts of *The Westminster Confession*, to which a member was expected to subscribe, even if he found some other parts unacceptable. The Special Committee anent the Doctrine of the Church (1969) described the substance of the faith as the irreducible minimum of belief, adherence to which was required for any church to claim to be part in the Catholic and Universal Church. Efforts have been made to express the substance of the faith in precise terms but it is difficult to secure agreement. Does it include features special to the Church of Scotland or is it as 'amorphous' as the 1969 committee suggested? The Panel on Doctrine in their 1984 report on *The Westminster Confession of Faith* said that Article 1 of the Declaratory Articles was as near as the church had come to a definition of the substance of the faith. The Assembly has however rejected Article 1 as an adequate summary of the faith. All this does not mean that the concept of the substance of the faith should be rejected as too elusive. It is easier to test whether some individual tenet can be described as being in accord with the substance of the faith than to secure agreement on a comprehensive definition of the substance.

Retention of *The Westminster Confession*

It is fashionable to decry *The Westminster Confession*, because in various respects it is out of tune with modern sentiments. We ought, however, to remember the services which it has rendered to the Church of Scotland and to world-wide presbyterianism over a long period of time, because this may be relevant to the question whether we need a modern version. *The Westminster Confession* helped to mould Scottish character into the shape we know. Armed with it, the Church of Scotland carried out a highly effective missionary operation in the Highlands in the 18th and early 19th centuries and helped to spread presbyterianism throughout the English speaking world. Reformed Scotland has never suffered from a heresy that split the Church; and throughout the divisions of the 18th and 19th centuries, all branches of the Church remained faithful to *The Westminster Confession*. It has survived sustained criticisms over a great many years. This is no mean record.

In various ways the Shorter Catechism, based on the Confession, now belongs to the past, but we should never forget our debt of gratitude to those 17th century divines who were prepared to devote their minds and hearts to preparing documents, like the Shorter Catechism, which stated, with brilliance and clarity, the essentials of doctrine as they understood them, in a form suitable for the ordinary man.

In the latter part of the 19th century, the task of revising *The Westminster Confession* seemed so formidable that the Church of Scotland, the Free Church and the United Presbyterians resorted to interpretations and conscience clauses. This was understandable because it is no easy affair to amend the Confession in detail. It represents a closely argued and closely knit body of doctrine. In 1903, the Presbyterian Church in the USA added two chapters on the Holy Spirit and on the Love of God and the need for Mission. It did not attempt to amend Chapter III on predestination but it made a declaratory statement that Chapter III was to be held to be in harmony with God's love for all mankind and with his readiness to bestow his saving grace on all who seek it. The declaratory statement, taken with Chapter III, was usually regarded as having created a confused situation.

There are a number of arguments in favour of retaining *The Westminster Confession*, apart from its inherent merits.

The least appealing is that there are what may be termed legal difficulties. It has been argued that any abandonment of the Confession would require Parliamentary authority on the ground that the Acts, including the Act of Union of 1707, which described *The Westminster Confession* as the principal subordinate standard of the Church of Scotland may not have been effectively abrogated by the Church of Scotland Act 1921. More serious is the argument that the Declaratory Articles contemplated revision and amendment of *The Westminster Confession* but not complete abandonment. These points would be pressed by those who are unwilling, for whatever reason, to see the Confession jettisoned.

Then, the great themes of the Confession have a special relevance today. *The Times* religious affairs correspondent on 30 December 1985 had the story of the visit of a group of clergymen to the City of London. The spokesman for the clergyman asked how they, the church, could be of service. He mentioned industrial chaplaincies, guidance on the ethics of investment and the morality of certain business practices. The clergymen were somewhat nonplussed when they received the answer: 'Tell us about God'.

Even the Confession's awesome portrayal of God as a God of authority, as well as of love, is badly needed today. Jesus portrayed a loving Father, ready to forgive the penitent sinner; but he expressed strict views on personal conduct and he foresaw a Day of Judgment. The soft and flabby presentation of Christianity in relation to personal religion is one of the great weaknesses of the Church. There is a tough side which is played down. The authors of the Wayside Pulpit think that it is enough to reiterate endlessly that God is Love. Those who eye the Church with doubts and misgivings need to be told where we stand on a number of issues including:

1 Do we believe in original sin and in the inability of man to reach moral perfection by his own efforts?
2 Do we believe that only a proportion of mankind will be saved and enjoy eternal life?
3 Do we believe that salvation can come only through Christ?
4 Do we believe, as a general proposition, that Christ taught absolute standards and not standards conditioned by the circumstances of His day?

It is prevarication or silence on some of these issues that makes the Church seem irrelevant. As the late Dean Matthews of St Paul's once wrote – 'The Gospel is a message of redemption and forgiveness and speaks in an unknown tongue to those who feel that they have done nothing to require forgiveness and no need of redemption.'

Christ's teaching is clear on these issues and *The Westminster Confession* is clear. Endeavouring to come to terms with humanism and influenced by Marxist thought and anxious to avoid saying anything that might by a side wind jeopardise the endless but unfruitful search for organic unity, the Church does not speak with an equally clear voice.

As Dr Sinclair Ferguson pointed out in his contribution to *The Westminster Confession in the Church Today*, the theology of a covenant of grace made by God with men seemed dead but has now taken on new meaning. 'In a striking way, the issues which caught the imagination of the 17th century are capturing the minds of Christians in the twentieth century'.

If we accept that *The Westminster Confession* will continue for some substantial time to be the Church's subordinate standard, then the Church ought to consider how to remove misconceptions to which it gives rise. It would be comparatively easy to add a chapter, on the American model, on the working of the Holy Spirit and on the need for evangelical mission. The spiritual independence of the Church should also now be affirmed, using the wording of the Articles. Double predestination presents a greater problem because of the closely knit nature of the Confession. If it is proclaimed that grace is available to all (as Chapter VII,3 seems to say) and if it is recognised that God is not bound by time as we know it (or think that we know it) then predestination becomes less of a problem and rather man's tribute to the majesty and greatness of God. A conscience clause will still be required on matters not coming within the substance of the faith. The Church has lived for long without any precise definition of what that substance is.

IV

The Word and the Sacraments

The ordinary church member's view on doctrinal matters is being distorted by the ecumenical discussions. These discussions tend to focus on disagreement between the churches on points of doctrine, as in the concentration in the Lima document on *Baptism, Eucharist and Ministry*. In understanding the doctrinal position of a church, the balance between the items of doctrine is important. The ecumenists analyse minutely the interpretation of the Lord's Supper by Reformed Churches, but little attention is paid to the balance between the Lord's Supper and other means of grace. The Reformed position is that the reading of the Scriptures and prayer and preaching are more important than the sacraments. As Francois Wendel said in his authoritative *Life of Calvin*:

> From the beginning (of the Institutes) the Gospels and the sacraments are treated in parallel, which does not mean, however, that Calvin puts them on the same plane. On the contrary, throughout his teaching he insisted upon the secondary and supplementary character of the sacraments, whereas the Gospel could be sufficient of itself in case of need, and expect normally to be so, were it not for our weakness which makes us dependent on cruder kinds of assistance.

Faith has to be implanted in the human soul. The Lord's Supper strengthens, but does not create, faith. It is erroneous to say that the Lord's Supper is the principal means of grace. It is erroneous to say that the communion table should have precedence over the pulpit.

One of the great problems facing Reformed churches today is this balance between the Word and the Sacraments, and it is of vital importance in the Church of Scotland. The present trend is to exalt the sacraments at the expense of reading, teaching and preaching the Word. This is evident from the Lima document. Sadly it is also evident from documents emanating from Church of Scotland committees. This trend must be reversed. This is not a specifically Scottish or presbyterian problem, although it arises particularly acutely in Scotland because preaching has always held so pre-eminent a place in Scottish presbyterianism.

We feel broad-minded when an invitation is extended to members of any branch of Christ's Church to participate in a Church of Scotland celebration of the Lord's Supper. What we should not forget, in proposals for frequent celebrations, is that we are saying 'Keep out of our services' to the vast army of people who are not members of any church.

Importance of preaching

Preaching of the Word is addressed to all whereas a sacrament is restricted to those in the particular denomination concerned or at best to those already in some branch of the Church. An outward-looking faith requires preaching. As Paul said to the Corinthians on one occasion – 'Christ sent me, not to baptise but to preach the Gospel'.

To the Reformers the mark of the true Church was the pure preaching of the Gospel. This was true of the Lutherans, as of John Calvin. *The Scots Confession of 1560* said that 'the notes of the true kirk of God we believe, confess and avow to be first, the true preaching of the Word of God, in which God has revealed Himself to us ...'. *The Second Helvetic Confession* said 'The preaching of the Word of God *is* the Word of God. Wherefore when this Word of God is now preached in the Church by preachers lawfully called, we believe that the very Word of God is proclaimed, and received by the faithful, and that neither any other Word of God is to be invented nor is to be expected from heaven ...'. *The Westminster Confession* likewise extols 'sound preaching'.

As the Special Committee on the Doctrine of the Church said in 1969, 'preaching remains, as it has always been, the chief means of communicating the Gospel.' The Falkirk investigation of 1968 to 1971 was only one of many illustrations of the fact that Church of Scotland congregations value, above all else, a faithful exposition of the Gospel message. After examining various difficulties about preaching in existing conditions, the Panel on

Doctrine in their 1973 report summed up its views as follows:

> The Panel is quite unshaken, therefore, in its stand with the Re-
> formers on the necessity, and on the uniquely direct communica-
> tive power, of preaching, however truly other speech-forms may
> also convey the Word; and, having pursued the questions raised
> by the [Priorities of Mission] Commission, we remain confident
> of the propriety of its form, and of the majority of our Church
> members' continuing recognition of the sermon as central and
> vital in the public worship of God and in their reception of His
> Word.

In the Reformed tradition, we speak of the Word and sacraments; and the reading and exposition of the Scriptures is the
more usual channel of grace than the sacraments. This is one of
the fundamental differences between the Roman Catholic and
the Reformed faith.

Efforts to belittle the differences between the Roman Catholic
and the Reformed view of the Lord's Supper stem, at least in
some measure, from attempts to upset the balance between
preaching and the sacraments. Of course it is said that preaching
would continue with a weekly or more frequent celebration of the
sacrament (the Lima document speaks of celebration at least
once a week), but Anglican experience shows that a weekly
celebration leads to a lowering of the standard of preaching. If
the sacrament is the more important, preaching will suffer, as
ministers will not put the necessary work into the preparation of
their sermons.

The Protestant churchgoer, when he can give effect to his
views, has resisted too frequent celebrations of the sacrament. It
was so in Calvin's day: it is so in the Church of Scotland today.
In England, the emphasis on the Eucharist at the expense of
preaching, has led to a massive fall in attendances at Church of
England places of worship.

James Moffatt in his Shaffer Lectures at the Divinity School of
Yale University recounted the story[1] of a Jesuit in Paris who said
to an audience 'Suppose that Jesus came holding in one hand the
eucharist and in the other the Gospels and said to you "I give you
the choice – my person in the Host or the story of my life in the
Book – which do you prefer?" The Jesuit said that he would
answer "Lord, since I cannot have both treasures at once, keep
your eucharist and give me the Gospels."' The importance of

preaching was well expressed some years ago by Dr Edward Woods, Bishop of Lichfield, a man of strong evangelical faith and a persuasive broadcaster. He wrote:

> These are times when the Ministry of the Word takes on a new significance and is charged with fresh potentialities. It is a grievous mistake at any time, and at the present time it is disastrous, for the Church's leaders and spokesmen to exalt the Ministry of the Sacraments at the expense of the Ministry of the Word. Preaching and teaching, prepared with meticulous care, based on deep thought and wide reading, and charged with the power won in the secret place of prayer, is not 'mere utterance', it is powerful to change the hearts of men and, indirectly but very really, to affect the course of history.[2]

Reference has already been made to a recent study[3] of the state of Anglicanism in country districts (always presumed to be its heartland) which gives a distressing picture of empty churches. *The Times* religious affairs correspondent spoke of towns of 8000 inhabitants where 15 would ordinarily attend the parish church. Of churches that were visited, a summary said:

> Six of the sermons were rated interesting, ten as dull and boring and the other services had none at all – the majority of clergy had apparently 'given up trying' in their preachings, for their sermons related neither to the service nor to life.

Professor W R Fryer, in a comment on the study, attributed the decline in attendances to the replacement of Mattins and Evensong by the celebration of the Eucharist.

Effective preaching requires careful preparation and a clear view on the way in which some aspect of the Gospels can be vividly presented. As Whately put it – preach, not because you have to say something, but because you have something to say. It was sometimes complained of the old-style preachers that they repeated their sermons: some modern sermons have so little original material in them and so little structure that they can be repeated again and again without the fact being noticed.

It is not true that good preaching is an intellectual exercise addressed to middle-class congregations. Principal George Hill of St Mary's College, St Andrews was a teacher of Thomas Chalmers, and it was said of his sermons:

The views which they unfolded made them interesting to the learned audience before which he preached; and yet their train of thought was so natural, and so perspicuously expressed, that the humblest of his hearers listened to him with profit and delight.

The same could be said of John Kelman who attracted vast congregations with sermons which also appealed to connoisseurs of the art like the fifth Lord Rosebery, one-time Prime Minister. These sermons were based on wide reading and assiduous preparation.

Sacraments

There is a growing tendency to represent God's saving grace as channelled through the sacraments. The minister who presides over the sacraments then becomes, as the purveyor of God's grace, in effect the controller of God's grace. This is utterly repugnant to Scriptural teaching. God operates through many channels in bestowing his grace – prayer, the reading of the Scriptures, preaching and other means.

The Church of Scotland regards the sacraments as important but not as essential for salvation.[4] *The Westminster Confession of Faith* says that outside the Church there is 'no ordinary possibility of salvation'. The word 'ordinary' acknowledges that, while God has bound us to the use of certain means, he is not himself bound. In regard to baptism, the Confession says that 'grace and salvation are not so inseparably annexed unto it as that no person can be regenerated or saved without it'.

A great deal of the imagery used in the past, has little meaning for the present generation of church members. A child brought up on the Shorter Catechism would accept a description of baptism as involving an 'ingrafting into Christ', but it comes fresh to a present-day member and can sound exceedingly strange. The ecumenists have avoided precise statements on doctrinal issues lest they create difficulties in inter-church negotiations: and we are now reaping the fruits of their vagueness and ambiguities.

Baptism

In the sacrament of baptism, the individual is admitted into the fellowship of the Church and, in the case of infant baptism, the parents promise to bring up the child in the Christian faith.

All the other meanings attached to baptism are derivative from admission to the fellowship of the Church. Thus, in so far as the Church may be described as the body of Christ, baptism can be described as 'ingrafting into Christ'. In so far as Christians 'partake of the benefits of the covenant of grace', baptism gives the promise of remission of sins for those who remain faithful to Christ.

Some negative points should be noted:

1 Baptism, although eminently desirable, is not essential to salvation, just as salvation may exceptionally be achieved without membership of the Church.

2 Baptism does not remit all sins previously committed, nor all sins to be committed in the future. Calvin refers to individuals who postponed baptism till they were on their death-bed, in the belief that the rite would make a clearance of all their sins. The Emperor Constantine was one such.

3 Baptism does not confer all the benefits of church membership, since full membership (including admission to the Lord's Supper) depends on a personal commitment to Christ by those who have reached an age at which such a commitment can be sought and given.

If too much weight is placed on baptism and on the effects of baptism – for example, in relation to admission to the Lord's Supper – there will be a rift in the Church. There is a widespread and understandable view that admission to full membership should involve personal commitment. In 1976 an overwhelming number of presbyteries indicated to the Special Committee anent Church Membership that they considered that personal profession of faith was an essential prerequisite to admission to communion and so to full membership. The number of members who sympathise with the Baptist view of baptism will grow if we do not keep, as a reality, admission by confession of faith at the adult stage. Baptism should not be treated as a magical rite.

The Lord's Supper

The most probable interpretation of the Last Supper is that it was a Passover meal and that Christ was indicating the form of Passover meal that his followers should conduct after he had gone. The meal would commemorate his death and resurrection in place of the successful flight from Egypt. Elements representing his body and blood would take the place of the Passover elements. His hearers may well have assumed that he contemplated an annual commemoration, like the Passover.

Roman Catholics would accept that Christ's sacrifice was made, once and for all, on the Cross: but they hold to the view that the elements become the body and blood of Christ, which can be reserved and worshipped. The Reformed view is that the bread and wine, though used for a holy purpose, remain bread and wine.

The Holy Spirit is present in the world at all places and at all times. The Spirit is present to hear the believer's prayers at home, at place of work, or in the open air. The Spirit is present during the reading and preaching of the Word, also when the Lord's Supper is celebrated. Is the Holy Spirit present in some special way during the celebration of the Lord's Supper? If so is this objectively or in the mind of the Church member? Is there some spiritual link with the bread and wine or is the link with the act of celebration or with the congregation assembled to participate? Calvin had views on these issues, which are not always easy to understand, but he also confessed that they raised questions which might be beyond human comprehension. Calvin rendered valuable service in drawing attention to the spiritual presence of the Holy Spirit. Zwingli had the insight that the work of the Holy Spirit is in the assembled congregation, as the body of Christ – members of a congregation which partake of the bread and wine are in communion with Christ.

Chapter XXIX of *The Westminster Confession* is as good a summary of the Reformed position, as we are likely to find. We have to be able to accommodate those who consider that Christ meant that the elements signified his body and blood and those who – while wholly agreeing that the bread and wine remain bread and wine – wish with Calvin to associate the Holy Spirit with the elements. We cannot maintain the necessary balance and Reformed comprehensiveness if we are trying to find formulae that attempt to reconcile the Reformed and Roman Catholic views. This is the danger presented by the Lima document and by *Christian Unity – Now is the Time*. The description of the Lord's Supper as 'the re-presentation of the sacrifice of Christ' is intended to reconcile the irreconcilable: and by no stretch of imagination can 'the reservation of the consecrated bread and wine' be blandly treated as presenting 'no theological disagreement sufficient to justify the perpetuation of our divisions'.

If Christ is present in a special way at the Lord's Supper and if the Lord's Supper is the principal channel of grace, then this leads logically to very frequent celebration – weekly or daily or hourly. On this, the attitude of the generality of church members has its own lesson. *Vox populi, vox dei*. They have been content to attend communion twice a year or thereabouts. From the time of Calvin onwards, they have resisted efforts to have more frequent celebrations. In recent times, the pressure for more frequent celebrations has come from ministers anxious to fall more closely in line with denominations which exalt the sacraments at the expense of the preaching of the Word.

Infrequent communions have the advantage of enhancing the importance of the occasion and of bringing together a larger proportion of the congregation. As already mentioned, Zwingli recognised the importance of the assembled congregation in the celebration of the Lord's Supper. A packed Church of Scotland congregation participating in a half-yearly service is an uplifting experience.

In the Church of Scotland, the Lord's Supper can be conducted only by a minister but that is for reasons of good order and discipline and not because he possesses any special power to distribute God's grace.

Virgin birth and resurrection

In recent discussions, arising out of views expressed by the Bishop of Durham, the Virgin Birth and the Resurrection have tended to be linked together; but in fact they are distinct and should be considered separately.

Conception by the Holy Spirit and the virgin birth were not part of the preaching of the apostles as recorded in the New Testament. They are described only in the first two chapters of Matthew and Luke and are not referred to again in these Gospels nor in the other two Gospels nor the letters of Paul, Peter, John nor the other letters. And of course Matthew gives Joseph's pedigree back to David and the first chapter of Romans refers to the Son of God as 'descended from David according to the flesh'. The Virgin Birth raises problems about the human manhood of Christ: failure to believe in the Virgin Birth raises problems at what point of time God took human form. Belief in the Virgin Birth is not of the substance of the faith.

The Resurrection is a different matter altogether. Belief in the resurrection of Christ, bodily and spiritually, is surely of the substance of the faith.

Notes and references to Chapter IV

1 Pinard de la Boallaye, H. *Jesus et l'Histoire*, p180ff, quoted by Moffatt, James (1942). *Jesus Christ the Same*. Hodder & Stoughton, p80.
2 *The Times*, 12 January 1953.
3 Francis, Leslie J (1985). *Rural Anglicanism*. Collins.
4 Henderson, G D (1948). *The Nature of the Church*. Aberdeen University Press, p5.

V

Members, Ministers and Elders

General

One of the advantages of departing from the ecumenical movement in the shape it has taken is that we can also put aside its obsession with an elaborate church structure.

We need to arm the individual Christian with the right ideas on his religion and to have the simplest practicable organisation for the Church. We need to get as near as we can to the simplicity of the early church which made its most vital advances when organisation was in its most rudimentary form.

Christianity was at the outset a lay movement. In the New Testament the term priest *(hiereus)* is used to refer to the priesthood of Christ and to the derivative priesthood of the whole people of God, but is never used to refer to an appointed Christian minister. The closest analogy to the ministry of the early church was the eldership of the synagogue.[1]

St Paul did not know of the existence of a 'ministry' in the sense in which we use that term today. There was no such thing as a uniform, universally recognised ministry in his day. There was no distinction between clergy and laity, for there was no clergy. As Professor R P C Hanson has pointed out, this conclusion of scholarship is not likely to be overturned in the foreseeable future.

It follows that no system of church government is prescribed in the Scriptures. As the Lima document puts it:

> The New Testament does not prescribe a single pattern of ministry which might serve as a blueprint or continuing norm for all future ministry in the Church. In the New Testament there appears rather a variety of forms that existed at different places and times.

Any argument that some feature of the organisation of churches – for example, the historic episcopacy – is to be regarded as an essential feature of the Church has, therefore, no scriptural warrant.

The Scriptures refer to the ministry of the whole people of God, and within that community the inference must be that any distinction between individuals is one of functions, not of status. This is the bedrock on which any 'theology' of church government should be based. Obviously there have to be guiding principles in the construction of any system of church government, but they should be based in large measure on practical and not on theological considerations. Past experience is useful, especially in relation to circumstances resembling our own. For this reason, recent experience since the Reformation is more valid than experience before the Reformation. We, as Protestants, eye warily tradition in pure theology: we must not admit it uncritically in matters of church government. We must beware of 'theological' concepts of organisation which often are no more than an attempt to give a spurious cover to preconceived ideas about the organisation of the Church. The Interim Report on Ministry by the Panel on Doctrine seems to provide an example of this. Christ's work on earth can be analysed in many ways. The Panel erects a theoretical structure on a division of Christ's ministry into proclamation and service, and then assumes that this should be reproduced in the organisation of the church. This is assumption piled on assumption. The Panel ends up by identifying proclamation with the ordained ministry and service with the eldership. Consciously or unconsciously, the train of thought may have begun by labelling the office-bearers and working from that. The whole process is of course devoid of scriptural authority. The initial error is in assuming that there must be a so-called 'theological' basis for church organisation, other than that all members of the church are equal and all are sinners.

After the Apostles, the church might have been organised as a loose federation on a congregational basis. For better or for worse it was not so organised. Why a hierarchical structure of bishops, priests and deacons developed is still a subject of debate. The threat of persecution has been advanced as a cause, but perhaps we should not forget what Bismarck once called 'the age-old struggle for power, as old as the human race itself'. Gibbon in *Decline and Fall* had no doubt that this was a major factor. The third epistle of John refers to Diotrephes 'who loveth to have the pre-eminence'. When it is said that the Church is in constant need of reformation, one of the main human traits that has to be corrected is the desire of individuals, whether ordained ministers or ecclesiastical bureaucrats, to exercise authority beyond the needs of the situation and often against the real interest of the Church as an instrument of evangelisation.

There is a sense in which presbyterians, living in Scotland, are not the best judges of the merits and demerits of the presbyterian system. They know no other, accept its merits as a matter of course and may be aware only of shortcomings.

There is immense value in a form of government which is pervaded with the knowledge that, under Christ, it is the members of the Church who matter and which therefore imbues in its members a strong sense that, under Christ, the Church is theirs, something to be cherished and developed.

There is also immense value in a form of government that is built on the foundation that there is no more important element in a church than the local congregation, that there is no more important minister than the minister of that congregation, and that representatives of the membership have an equal vote with ministers in the upper courts of the church on all matters that come before these courts.

In considering how the Church of Scotland should develop in its organisation, it is necessary to look first at the wider scene.

All churches accept that the whole people of God should be regarded as exercising a ministry; and all churches, including the Roman Catholic Church, go further and accept the importance of the local congregation of the faithful. St Paul's description of the church as the Body of Christ is endlessly developed – perhaps, as Professor G D Henderson once hinted, over-developed.

However, as the Panel on Doctrine in their Interim Report on the Ministry (1985) pointed out: 'Too hastily the axiom that ministry belongs to the whole common membership of Christ's one Body makes way for near-exclusive focus on the recognition and ordering of special ministries'.

Thus, in practice, the ecumenical movement sees the ordained ministry as the key feature in the church. Ecumenists assume that the ordained ministry of any united church would be organised in the three-fold order of bishop, priest (or presbyter) and deacon. While this is the traditional description of the organisation of episcopal churches, it is one of the oddities of the

ecumenical movement that it should lay such store on the diaconate (described in the Lima document as representing the
church in its calling as servant in the world) in view of the indis-
putable fact that the deacon has never had any secure position in
the Roman Catholic or Anglican hierarchy. Indeed in the recent
past there have been proposals in the Church of England for the
abolition of the office. As recently as 1985, the Church of England's Board for Mission and Unity remarked that in spite of
repeated calls that this should be done, little attempt had been
made to clarify the meaning of the diaconate. In the Anglican
Church the diaconate has afforded newly trained clergy a short
period of probation and preparation for the priesthood. Until
such time as women are admitted to the priesthood of the Church
of England, their admission to the Anglican diaconate introduces
a more permanent element to the diaconate. It is, however, a
subordinate grade in a clerical hierarchy to which women can be
admitted without arousing 'Catholic' objections to the ordination of women priests. It is also a grade with no clear role in the
government of the church.

In the Church of England, the General Synod is organised in
'houses' – bishops, clergy and laity. On matters of any importance the houses vote separately. A majority (or sometimes a
two-thirds or three-quarters majority) in each house must be
obtained. In effect, therefore, the bishops and clergy have a
separate veto on change.

Against this general background it is now necessary to examine how the matter of church organisation is being currently
handled in the Church of Scotland.

The Panel on Doctrine in its Interim Report on the Ministry
(1985) sets out the view that the ministry of all members of the
church means the repudiation of the contrast between 'clerical'
and 'lay' and the assignment of no special status to ordained
ministers apart from the function of ensuring that the worship,
evangelism and mission of the whole church is well-ordered and
faithful. The Panel says of the ministry of Word and sacrament,
'they comprise no separate order, their status is no higher or
lower than that of any of Christ's loved ones, their function is to
see, on behalf of the whole Body, that the privilege and task of all
is done with order – that with love and constancy, preparation
and discernment, the good news entrusted to the church is handed round and handed on in word and water, bread and wine'.

Alas! All this is watered down when the Panel tries to reconcile its more robust thoughts with the stock-in-trade of the ecumenists.

The ministry exercised by the church member becomes the ministry of the baptised and therefore capable of being performed by a child of two. Admission by public profession of faith is referred to in what is almost a parenthesis, and no attempt is made to relate baptism to profession of faith. The Panel never gets beyond vague statements about the duties and responsibilities of individual members.

As regards the ordained ministry, the Panel assumes 'appropriate endowments' of the Holy Spirit to ministers of Word and sacrament, so that the ministry might secure the obedience of the whole. One has reached the concept of the ordained ministry, divinely selected, as exercising the ministry of the whole people of God and 'overseeing the obedience of the whole'. The ministry of the whole people thus becomes little more than a theoretical concept, with few practical consequences. The assumption of special injections of the Holy Spirit is unwarranted and at variance with the functional concept of the ordained ministry.

As regards the eldership, the Panel clearly draws on the ecumenical office of deacon to create its ministry of service. The report of the Multilateral Conversation made an explicit link between the deacon and the elder. One would have thought that anyone with respect for the eldership would have drawn back from creating links with an office which is subordinate in character to the ordained ministry and has no defined place in the government of the church. Elders are to be bundled into the so-called ministry of service, along with deaconesses (and male deacons) and various other church workers, including no doubt members of congregational boards. The Panel shows a preference for elders being commissioned rather than ordained, thus emphasising the higher status of the ordained ministry of Word and sacrament. The elder's vital role in the government of the church is not thought worthy of consideration. The Panel asks the rhetorical question: 'And is then their leadership in service and pastoral care, rather than their rule and power, the true mark and source of their authority?' On the question whether the elder is being put in a subordinate position, the best that the Panel can present is the following flow of words:

What gives this ministry of service significance and power and prevents the subordination of those charged with *Diakonia* to those entrusted with *Kerygma*, is the fact that human obedience to the Word of God is God's own possibility, a gift of grace made real for us in the divine humility of Christ's humanity.

If the foregoing has any meaning, it has defied my best efforts to extract it. The truth is that the hierarchy of bishop, presbyter and deacon, or any two parts of that hierarchy, are incompatible with presbyterianism. No amount of verbiage can get round the fact that the concepts would be interpreted as involving the subordination of one grade to another, and this would radically change, for the worse, the Church of Scotland as we know and love it.

Members

A member of the church is chosen by God to fulfil his role, quite as much as the ordained minister, and he is answerable to God for his actions. Luther expressed the idea as the priesthood of all believers. Calvin did not use the phrase, though he shared with Luther the belief in the importance of the individual member who is chosen by God. Zwingli had the sense of the divine presence in the congregation of the faithful. The divine call to the individual Christian is as a member of the church and not in a way that would leave every Christian free 'to do his own thing'. A child at baptism becomes a part of the church but does not become fully involved in the duties of membership until he is admitted to full membership as he approaches adulthood. Young people do not have the vote in parliamentary or local elections or liability to jury service till they reach the age of 18. The responsibilities of presbyterian church membership are, or should be, equally onerous and should be undertaken about the same age on public profession of faith. The individual members are the base on which the organisation of the church is constructed and from which, under God, the higher courts derive their authority.

It is essential to involve the individual members of the church in the work of the church. Church people need something definite to do, something that will bring out their capabilities and promote the exercise of their gifts. This renders fellowship interesting and action rewarding.

A member carries his Christian responsibilities into spheres not controlled by the Church. The Committee of Forty regarded any activity that ceased to be carried out by the Church as involving 'secularisation'. This is a false antithesis. The Church cannot cover the many activities now carried out beneficially by public authorities. It is the duty of members of the Church, as electors or members of these bodies, to endeavour to secure that they have regard to Christian principles in their administration. It is the responsibility of the Church to inculcate Christian principles in its members but not in the ordinary way to profess to apply these principles to particular situations. That is the business of the individual Christians involved in administration and aware of the many factors that have to be considered. Their sense of responsibility can be eroded if the Church tries to do their job for them. More has been done in this world by individual Christians applying their Christian beliefs to situations that needed correction than by all the resolutions passed by church assemblies.

Within the Church itself, everything should be done to increase in the Church member the sense of responsibility and the sense of 'belonging'. All accept this in theory but it is not carried through in practice.

Nothing should be done to detract from the rights of church members to choose their minister. Attempts to secure what some central body, probably composed largely of ministers, regards as the most efficient use of resources must take second place. In any event, ministers are often indifferent judges of the preaching and pastoral gifts of a colleague, though they may know his views and prejudices and his performance in presbytery and assembly.

Elders should in all cases be elected by the congregation. Congregational boards should consist largely of directly elected members, so as to secure the widest spread of members engaged in administering the affairs of the church.

The habit of encouraging general contributions to the funds of the church, with allocations made at 121 George Street, should be abandoned. Members should be encouraged to allocate their contributions to individual funds. The belief that 'George Street knows best' does not assist the development of a responsible membership.

Kirk Sessions should be more ready to seek the views of the congregation on current issues, either by a questionnaire sent to all members or at a congregational meeting. Congregational meetings are often poorly attended. Arousing and sustaining the interest of the congregation may be a slow process but the effort should be made and persevered with.

There may well be fundamental issues on which it would be desirable to have a vote by all church members. If the Reformers had had our ease of communication, surely they would have used it to involve the whole membership in the running of the church. In fact, in the involvement of the membership as a whole in important matters, we have sometimes moved backward. For example, the Barrier Act in its earliest form (1639) required reference on substantial issues to kirk sessions as well as to presbyteries. If alterations are proposed in the Declaratory Articles, this at present requires the approval of two Assemblies and approval by two thirds of the presbyteries. There could be an additional requirement of approval by two thirds of those voting in a referendum to church members. A reference of fundamental issues to the entire church membership would show that ultimate authority lies there. A move in this direction would encourage ministers to aim at developing a knowledgeable membership, such as existed in the past to a greater extent than at present. As things are at present, the person-in-the-pew cannot vote against a proposed innovation, but he can always stay away – and only too often does.

Ruling elders
As already indicated, questions about the organisation of the church are practical matters. Within certain principles, how can the church be most effectively organised? We should look first at the large numbers and the large blocks of work. This means first attention to members, ministers, elders and members of congregational boards. The organisation should not revolve round the place of 50 deacons and deaconesses. The main structure should be got right and then the deaconesses and others can be fitted in.

On 31 December 1986, there were about 850 000 communicant members in Scotland, 1300 ministers serving charges, 47 500 elders and 20 000 other office-bearers (members of congregational boards and the like). In addition there were about 70 probationers and 50 deaconesses. Are the present duties of these individuals properly arranged or should they be changed?

The ruling elder is an essential feature of the Church of Scotland as a presbyterian church. In the past a recommendation for its adoption by other churches has been a feature of ecumenical discussions from the 17th century onwards. Principal Burleigh prepared a note on the eldership for the conversations which resulted in the Bishops Report. It concluded: 'Their office is in a broad sense spiritual and pastoral, distinct from but closely associated with the ministry of Word and sacrament, and to it they are solemnly set apart with a ceremony not unfittingly termed ordination'.

For the individual elder, the visiting of members in his district, participating in the work of the Kirk Session and assisting at the Lord's Supper constitute the main part of his duties. From the point of view of church government, the elder's main importance lies in the part he plays in all the courts of the church. As provided in the Basis and Plan of Union, 1929, there must be elders equal in number to the ministers in presbyteries, synods and the General Assembly. Subsequent legislation has had the effect of increasing the number of elders in the lower courts, so that today they outnumber ministers in presbytery and synod, only the General Assembly continuing to have complete parity. Further the elders participate on equal terms in all the business that comes before these courts, including doctrine, worship and discipline. Although elders do not lay on hands at the ordination of a minister or pronounce a sentence of excommunication or intimate a sentence and censure about a minister, they share in every step leading up to these formal acts.

Cox's *Practice and Procedure in the Church of Scotland* (sixth edition, 1976) states that all members of session are elders, ministers being teaching or preaching elders as well as ruling elders, the others being ruling elders only. Cox quotes the *Second Book of Discipline* when it says that 'the eldership is a spiritual function as is the ministry'. The distinction between minister and elder is simply that between teaching elder and ruling elder, and both are to be seen as sharing the status of presbyter or elder. Ruling elders are ordained and admitted by the Kirk Session. Ministers are ordained and inducted to a charge by the presbytery, to which they are accountable for the discharge of their duties.

The Reformed churches in the 16th century instituted the office of elder. In the long discussion on church government in the 17th century, Scots argued that the eldership was a Scriptural office and New Testament texts were quoted. As already indicated, there is now less conviction about any common pattern of organisation in the primitive church. Professor T F Torrance in *The Eldership in the Reformed Church* (1984) and elsewhere shows that the kind of ministry exercised by elders in the Reformed Church is not inconsistent with the outlook to be found in the New Testament, and the eldership bears a resemblance to the office and functions of deacons as described in the Epistles and early church documents. These historical parallels are of interest but are not of fundamental importance in organising church government in the 20th century. What is beyond question is that the eldership has proved a source of strength to the church for several hundreds of years. There are 47 500 elders in the Church of Scotland and much has been done to encourage the training of elders in their duties.

Everything must be done, and much is being done, to help and encourage the elder in his pastoral duties. But it is equally clear that his position in the courts of the church must be maintained. In this regard, the ecumenists within the Church of Scotland give the impression of being engaged in 'destabilising' the ruling function of the elder. Ruling elders who are empowered to take part in the church courts in all questions of doctrine, worship, discipline and government and who must at least equal ordained ministers in number in presbyteries, synods and assembly do not fit into the clerical control, or at least veto, which ecumenists tacitly assume as the norm. The description of the position of elders in the higher courts contained in the Bishops Report was obviously designed not to shock tender consciences in the Anglican communion. Thus the function of elders in the Assembly was not described as being to speak and vote on all issues but as to 'report back to the Session any business of special concern or interest to the particular parish'. It was with some difficulty that reference to the position of elders in the higher courts was introduced into the Panel's 1965 report on the eldership. Once again the subject was not adequately dealt with in the Panel's interim report on the ministry. The elder is told that he is to see his 'authority' in terms of service rather than of power. That of course is what the disgruntled clerics thought in 1638. It is also argued that all church workers are performing a spiritual task. This is misleading. Members of congregational boards are engaged in important duties in the church but they are not spiritual duties. If a bill for building work in a church or an electricity bill is not paid, the congregational board cannot say that this is a spiritual matter to be handled in the church courts. Congregational boards and their predecessors were set up to enable elders to concentrate on their spiritual functions. The Panel propose to downgrade the elder by commissioning him, rather than ordaining him. At least that seems to be the course that they prefer. It proposes to bracket him with other church workers in a ministry of service. The Panel describes this as giving fresh meaning and significance to the role of elders. As the Duke of Wellington said to the man who addressed him as Mr Smith, 'If you can believe that, you can believe anything'.

The position of the elder in the church could be eroded in these theoretical discussions which would eventually take practical form in a re-arrangement of the machinery of the church. There have been many discussions over the years about the status of the eldership. The church cannot afford to remain in doubt on this issue.

The eldership has to be judged by its past and present usefulness to the church. As envisaged in the *Second Book of Discipline*, the eldership should be linked with the ministry as engaged in a spiritual function, rather than with the members of congregational boards. It is essential that elders retain their present position in presbytery, synod and General Assembly. Fortunately, in the light of the comments of presbyteries on the report of the Multilateral Conversation, the 1986 Assembly affirmed that the eldership was central to the Church's ministry and government.

Ministry
Amid much ecumenical talk about the need to induce the members to play a more active part, it remains true that the ecumenical movement is clergy-led and interested above all else in the ministry and its organisation. This is a threat to the ethos of the Church of Scotland, where ministers have never claimed to be a separate caste or behaved like one. Ministers have often been closer to their elders than to other ministers.

Episcopacy
The threat to the organisation of the church takes specific form in the proposition that in the united church there should be the

threefold ministry of bishop, priest (or presbyter if that sounds less alarming) and deacon.

How distant any organisation based on the historic episcopacy is from our presbyterian ways of thought can be seen in a recent booklet entitled *The Power of the Bishop* (1987) by John Halliburton and on sale in Church of Scotland bookshops. The authority of the bishop derives from the apostolic succession of bishops and the authority of the priest is by delegation of authority from the bishop.

If the episcopate is said to be essential to the Church, one is entitled to examine the detailed grounds on which this claim is made. They do not bear close examination.

The bishops are supposed to be anchor-men who keep the Church attached to the faith. This is not necessarily so. Bishops in the Anglican communion fail to perform this task. This is so obvious that it does not need detailed proof. The Anglo-Catholics in the Church of England, who are specially strong on the need for episcopacy, are among the most vociferous critics of those Anglican bishops on whom traditional views hang somewhat lightly.

It is said that, at a higher level than the congregation, there is need for 'the prophetic role of discerning what needs doing that is not being done and of fostering new insights and new forms of service within the Church'. For this, many heads are better than one and there is no reason why the members of a presbytery should not be able to perform this function.

Then it is argued that there should be a personally-embodied means of strengthening the links between the local congregation and the wider Church. This seems to boil down to saying that, because there are bishops in some churches, there should be bishops everywhere, so that bishop can talk to bishop. This can hardly be sustained as a reason for abandoning our well-tried presbyterian system.

It is frequently argued that the presbyterian system is defective because of the lack of anyone in authority who can give guidance to a minister who is in difficulties of one kind or another. Bishops may be chosen for a variety of reasons. They may be chosen as competent administrators or as theologians but not necessarily or even ordinarily as father-figures. The problem of dealing with bewildered, cantankerous or erring clergymen should not be exaggerated. It is not common, but in so far as it exists it appears to perplex the Church of England, with its bench of bishops, quite as much as it does the Church of Scotland. Some Anglican dioceses have appointed pastoral advisers. Some presbyteries have committees to look after personal problems. Statistics about difficult Church of England clergy are not collected centrally, so there is no information on which accurate views could be formed on how the problem is tackled. As so often in the field of ecumenism, any claim in favour of episcopacy is merely an unsubstantiated assertion.

What the Church of Scotland must guard against is any step by step approach, starting with quasi-permanent moderators of presbyteries. As Dr Andrew Herron pointed out in his 1985 Baird Lectures, this is the road to the abandonment of the great advantages of parity of ministers.

David F Wright of New College, in some useful comments on the Multilateral Conversation, made an unfortunate suggestion that there might be regional ministers to deal with some questions of a wider character. Several presbyteries took up the idea in their answers to the Board of World Mission and Unity. The idea is fraught with trouble for the church. Regional ministers might be a practicable proposition in a church where everyone was a convinced presbyterian and the regional ministers were saints. In practice some of the regional ministers would yearn for more power and be continuously seeking it; and those who were episcopalians at heart would use the development to try to move towards episcopacy. There would be endless friction and endless unsettlement. We want no Trojan horse in our presbyterian structure.

The experience of the United Reformed Church shows how far and how quickly you can depart from the parity of ministers if any chink is opened. The Congregational Union had had some ministers who were given the task of assisting and advising churches, particularly the large number of small churches who at one time were without ministers. They had no constitutional status. They became part of the structure of the United Reformed Church in 1972 as moderators of the twelve provincial synods. They are currently appointed by the General Assembly for seven years, with power of extension and are responsible to the Assembly. They have no parochial charge and are expected 'to stimulate and encourage the work of the Church within the province' and to suggest names for vacant pastorates. The moderators meet regularly together. The proposal to appoint them caused alarm in 1971–72 among true-blue presbyterians but the advocates of the scheme said that they would be pastors at regional level and that any tendency towards prelacy would be impossible because of their relationship to the councils of the church.

Fairly or unfairly, there were soon allegations of episcopalian pretensions by the moderators: and certainly in their reports to the Assembly they said that they had to 'represent' the URC and 'relate' to bishops, chairmen and superintendents. In 1982, in connection with the Covenant, the moderators indicated that they would be happy to become bishops within the historic episcopate. The Covenant provided for the contingency that a provincial moderator might be unwilling to become a bishop, but that provision was obviously not going to be required. In effect the URC has suffered from creeping episcopalianism. Can any clearer indication be given of the danger of any departure from presbyterian parity?

If the Church is to bring back within the fold the churchless millions, it must have regard to their views and prejudices, in so far as they do not run counter to the substance of the faith. At the time of the Bishops Report, it was noticeable that there was strong support for presbyterianism outside the Church of Scotland. In an oft-quoted story, one outsider is reported to have said: 'I may be an agnostic, but I am a presbyterian agnostic'. To the average Scot, a minister who gives himself a fancy title and dresses up in fancy garb is just rather silly: and it all seems to have little relation to the religion that Christ taught. A Scot remembers the great figures in the history of the Scottish Church who were content to stand on an equality with their fellows and who secured pre-eminence by the force of their personality, their prophetic gifts and the purity of their lives. We do not, alas! recruit for the ministry so many among the intellectual flower of the nation as we did in the past, but that is no reason for attempting to give a few, by hierarchical ranks, a pre-eminence which is undesirable on other grounds.

The adoption of any form of episcopacy would destroy the Church of Scotland as we know it. A very substantial number of ministers, elders and members would refuse to abandon presbyterianism. The Church would be rent in twain, as at the time of the Disruption. Those who accepted episcopacy would find that the Church gradually lost all its traditional characteristics. The bishops would naturally be drawn from among those who favoured an Anglican pattern: and, by reason of their office, they would have the necessary power to ensure that there could be no return to presbyterianism. The Scottish mind does not take kindly to compromise, and there would be an inevitable polarisation between the many who remained presbyterian and the few who would eventually be absorbed in something like the Episcopal Church. But what controversy, what waste of energy, what hurt to the cause of Christ would be suffered in the process!

Ordained Ministers

Every branch of the Christian Church acknowledges the importance of the local congregation, though some denominations are more congregationally minded than others. As already mentioned, even a highly centralised organisation like the Roman Catholic Church accepts the importance of the local church. The Dogmatic Constitution of Vatican II, *Lumen Gentum*, says 'The Church of Christ is truly present in all legitimate local congregations of the faithful which, united with their pastors, are themselves called churches in the New Testament.'[2]

One of the great virtues of the presbyterian system is that it bases its organisation on the importance of the local unit. John Knox took the parish and its kirk session as the foundation upon which the whole structure was built and the Scottish church has never wandered far from this principle. Members are members of a congregation. No one in the church is held in higher esteem than the parish minister ministering to the local congregation and no-one in the structure is vested with more power than he.

Such a parish minister will normally have gone through six stages:-

1 He decides that he wishes to become a minister.

2 He is accepted after selection by an Assembly Committee and after nomination by his presbytery, and he studies for and gains certain necessary qualifications at a university.

3 His presbytery, after trials, licenses him as a preacher of the Gospel, and he serves a year's probationary training.

4 The members of a congregation decide to call him to be their minister.

5 The presbytery, consisting of ministers and elders, decide that

he should be commissioned as a minister and should be inducted to the charge.

6 The presbytery commissions him by ordination, consisting of prayer and the laying-on of hands by the ministerial members, and in the name of the Lord Jesus Christ and by authority of the presbytery he is inducted and becomes minister of the charge.

This process can be variously described. As an organisation, the church requires leaders. These leaders are described by St Paul as provided by God. This can be regarded as an application of Paul's general proposition that there is no authority but by act of God. God chooses those who are admitted to baptism or to full membership of the Church and those members who are chosen as elders. In like manner he chooses those who undertake the great responsibilities of the ministry.

One train of thought has to be resisted – that the ministry is a self-perpetuating body of individuals who, by the magical rite of ordination performed by ministers alone, secure a divine commission which can be traced back to the Apostles. Nor can one accept the statement, endorsed by the Panel on Doctrine in the Statement of Belief for Popular Use, that the distinctive mark of the Church is the ministry of Word and sacrament. The distinctive mark of the true Church is faithfulness to the Scriptures.

Ordination is the solemn setting apart of a person to a public church office. Ordination by the laying-on of hands has been continuous in the Church of Scotland since the earliest times; but the only continuity of enduring worth is faithfulness to the Scriptures. While the laying-on of hands illustrates the continuity of the Church, it ought not to be inferred that it is a magical rite which conveys authority. No doubt it was the fear of this that led the authors of the *Scots Confession* to propose (with what temporary success is not known) the abandonment of the laying-on of hands. Calvin saw it as showing to the people the dignity of the office of minister and reminding the ordained that he was no longer his own master but devoted to the service of God and the Church. It is a great tragedy if an act which was designed to bind the minister more firmly into the one great fellowship of the church has in fact the effect of setting him apart as one of a clique within the church.

In Scotland, what spiritual grace a candidate possesses is thought to be observable before his admission and not to be the product of the ordination ceremony. The imposition is not held to convey the gifts of the Holy Spirit but is a recognition and seal of spiritual gifts already present.

The distinction between a member admitted by profession of faith to the church and an office-bearer – be he minister, elder, member of congregational board or other officer – is one of function and not of status.

The call by the congregation should never be denigrated. It is an important element in the setting apart of a minister for his vocation. There has been a tendency to depart from the practice that a call was a condition precedent to ordination. Assistants should not be ordained until they have a charge, and it might be no bad thing if anyone intended for a special assignment had first to serve in a parish. All this would emphasise the importance of the call by a congregation.

We must stick by the *Second Book of Discipline* and consider ministers as teaching or preaching elders. They are to be accorded all due honour and support in the Lord but a Reformed church must eye with circumspection any attempt to give ministers priestly functions. The Panel on Doctrine in *Agreement and Disagreement* (1977) said:

> There are certain characteristically 'priestly' functions which are in fact carried out by ministers of the Church of Scotland – for example, the calling of the people to worship, the offering of prayers and the giving of the blessing from God. The difference in labels obscures important similarities in function.

There is a certain amount of confusion in this statement. The pre-eminence given to a minister means that he is the natural person to lead the congregation in public worship and to expound the Scriptures. These are not priestly functions.

Courts of the Church

The organisation of the church was the subject of prolonged examination by the Committee of Forty. Decisions were taken on a number of subjects, sometimes while the committee was still sitting. Where changes have been made, time is required to see how the new arrangements are working.

The extent to which the membership of the General Assembly changes from year to year is no new phenomenon. It existed in the 18th century as much as today. It has, however, particular disadvantages at a time when old standards have less authority and when opinions on many subjects are so fluid. However, presbyteries in 1977 turned down unanimously the idea of membership of the Assembly for a number of years; and, if they had not done so, that solution would have brought a new crop of problems.

The arrangements for nomination to Assembly committees might be improved, though the subject is a difficult one. Too many committees do not seem to reflect the real mind of the church, as it is revealed when proposals reach presbyteries. Committees should not consist solely or mainly of enthusiasts for change. Ministers and elders who are content with things as they are usually see no point in volunteering for service on, say, the Panel on Worship. Nevertheless, the convener and some other members could usefully be drawn from middle-of-the-road characters.

If the composition of the Assembly may be thought to change too much, the composition of some committees changes too little or at least their affiliations change too little. The Panel on Doctrine is a prime example. The original intention was that there should be a regular change of membership, to ensure that no one school of thought controlled the Panel. This was departed from. The Church needs to revert to the original scheme.

The prohibition of minority reports should be removed and in this way a minority should find it easier than at present to make its views known. All too frequently a report fails to present an objective view. This would be corrected if the Assembly also had a minority presentation. The permission to present minority reports would also encourage ministers and elders to serve on committees. At present those out of sympathy with the views of the majority find themselves more or less powerless and and are apt to resign from the committee in a feeling of frustration.

Some means needs to be devised by which reports to the Assembly on important issues are submitted to a more rigorous scrutiny than is provided by the present Assembly procedures. One possible course would be for committees drawn from Assembly members to examine the convener and other members of a board or committee before the discussion of a report in the Assembly; with power to inform the Assembly of any feature that required special scrutiny. At present reports have to be in the hands of the Assembly Clerk by early in February. As the original committee may not have got to work till the previous

October, it is not practicable to suggest that reports should be submitted at an earlier date, to enable any preliminary scrutiny to be undertaken. The solution might be to provide that on important issues a committee should be given more time and should not be expected to report to the next Assembly but to its successor.

There is a danger that the membership of presbyteries is enlarged by adding categories of members till they cease to be effective executive instruments. This needs to be watched.

Relations with the State

The Church of Scotland asserts that it has sovereign powers in spiritual matters, and the State in the Church of Scotland Act 1921 accepted this in full measure. The Church also asserts that it is the sole judge of what constitutes a spiritual matter, though the civil courts also claim to decide what is within their jurisdiction. In form all is well, and other churches envy the Church of Scotland for the acceptance of its independence which it has secured.

There is an implication in establishment that the population belongs in very substantial numbers to the Church of Scotland. There can then be a division of responsibilities between Church and State in respect of the people of Scotland. Any departure from the Reformed traditions of the Church of Scotland would cause a schism on the scale of the Disruption. Thereafter, as happened in the second half of the last century, disestablishment could become a live issue.

Meantime the Church should not relax its guard. There are dangers that surface from time to time.

House of Lords in its Judicial Capacity

If Scots Law was to be preserved in its pristine purity, the Treaty of Union of 1707 should have provided that there was to be no appeal in civil cases from the Court of Session to the House of Lords. The Treaty was silent on the point and cases were taken to the Lords. In respect of criminal cases, when a Court of Criminal Appeal was set up in 1926, it was expressly provided that there was to be no appeal to another Court.

Although there are Lords of Appeal drawn from Scotland, English law, or at least English attitudes of mind, can colour House of Lords decisions in Scottish cases. The Scottish view is that the courts of the Church of Scotland exist alongside the civil courts and that in spiritual matters, such as church discipline, there is no appeal to the civil courts on merit or pleas of irregularity. There has been a great development of administrative law in recent years and a considerable spread of the habit of appealing to the civil courts when it is alleged that some body has failed to observe natural justice in its conduct of business, especially in the disciplining of its members. One cannot be quite sure how the House of Lords would treat a case which reached it in which a member of the Church of Scotland appealed against a finding of a church court and alleged irregular conduct.

Circumstances have changed in many ways since the famous Free Church case of 1903–04, when the House of Lords in effect rejected the view that the Free Church of the Disruption should be regarded as a living church, able to change as conditions changed, not a 'dead branch' bound to the tenets of 1843. Nevertheless, no one can be sure what would be the outcome if the House of Lords had to adjudicate on the issue whether the Church of Scotland could cut adrift from the *Westminster Confession of Faith*.

All members of the Church of Scotland cherish its spiritual independence. No one should pursue a course, to gain some temporary advantage, which might lead to the scope of that independence being called in question.

House of Lords in its Legislative Capacity
From time to time it has been suggested, even on occasion by the Church and Nation Committee, that in any reform of the House of Lords an effort should be made to secure Church of Scotland representation in that Chamber.

The Church of Scotland as a presbyterian church never claimed representation in the Scots Parliament. In 1638 the General Assembly passed an Act which said that the Reformed church had never sought a vote in Parliament and that this had been obtruded upon it. The Assembly forbade any minister to sit in Parliament.

Members of the Church are to be found in both Houses of Parliament as Scots nominated in civil capacities. In what sense could any representatives be said to represent the Church? The Church speaks through its courts. If the General Assembly has delivered itself of a view on a public issue, the expression of opinion is there for all to see. Only if individuals are in a position of authority, such as bishops of the Church of England are considered to enjoy, could they purport to express a Church view on the miscellaneous mass of questions coming before Parliament.

But there is also a more fundamental objection. If Church and State ever come in conflict, it will probably be on some issue that is partly civil and partly spiritual. The Church may say that the issues are mainly spiritual and the State that they are mainly civil. In any disagreement of this kind, the position of the Church will be immensely weakened if it has accepted representation in the Civil Legislature. The State can say that the point of view of the Church was duly put forward in the Second Chamber but that the general vote was against it. The Church is in a stronger position if it deals with the State on the basis of one legislature (the General Assembly) dealing with another Parliament).

Notes and references to Chapter V

1 Church of England's Board for Mission and Unity (1986). *The Priesthood of the Ordained Ministry*. Church House Publishing, pp 17, 23 and 27.
2 Quoted at page 5 of the *Response of the RC Bishops Conference of England and Wales* (April 1985) to the *Final Report of the Anglo-Roman Catholic International Conference*.

VI

Church and Nation

General

It is the duty of a Christian to apply Christian principles to all his activities. Christianity covers every aspect of life. It is the duty of his Church to inculcate Christian principles in all its members, particulary the young. The great philanthropists of the 19th century, like Lord Shaftesbury, traced their zeal for reform to the Christian training that they had received in their youth and to their continuing Christian faith.

If matters are left on this basis, the influence of the Church (as distinct from its members) in political, social and economic matters is long-term and indirect, except on great moral issues when the Church must speak. There has, however, been a recent widespread tendency for Church authorities to go much further, not merely to draw attention to public evils that need to be corrected but to go on to recommend specific remedies. Or more often to support the remedies proposed by others, particularly political parties. Sometimes their zeal for specific nostrums has seemed to be a main feature in their proclamation of the faith. Is it for the individual Christian to make up his mind or can organs of the Church usefully express authoritative views on political, social and economic issues? The problem is in some ways more difficult for a presbyterian church than for churches in which individuals are given a special status and may claim to be empowered to expound the application of the faith. Whether in practice bishops and the like have proved to be capable of giving useful guidance is of course another matter.

The subject is divisible into two parts. There may be general agreement among the members of a Church that some activity is undesirable and that measures of some kind should be taken to stop or regulate it. The Church authorities may, however, take the further step of indicating what specific measures should be taken to stop or control the abuse. It is usually much more difficult to secure general agreement on what these measures should be.

We all know why the Churches have become involved in these issues. The sphere of activity of public authorities has enormously increased in recent years and affects the lives of individuals at almost every point. Inevitably there is a demand that the Church should express views on these activities, particularly as some of them were undertaken by the Church itself in former times. If Christianity seems to be an intensely personal religion, with emphasis on the after-life, then it is criticised as the opiate of the people – making people willing to endure injustices that they ought not to endure – and this allegation serves as a goad to spur the Churches to express views on material issues.

In practice, it is a matter of balance. It is often said unfairly that in the 19th century the Churches taught too individualistic a religion and ignored social evils. This is not true. Church leaders expressed themselves strongly on social questions, but the main thrust of their teaching related to eternity and to man's place in the divine order of things. The balance has swung too far in the other direction. The tendency of the Churches – as distinct from the individual Christian – to get involved in political issues has gone too far and is harming the Churches. Certainly there is need for a thorough examination of the whole matter.

Christ's teaching was directed at the conduct of the individual and aimed always at the spiritual root of the disease, never at the material symptoms. When asked about the division of an estate, Christ's answer was not a talk on a fair system of intestate succession but the advice to 'beware of covetousness'. He was not a social reformer in the sense of setting out a programme for the political, social and economic evils of the day. This should remind us of the ephemeral character of many of these programmes. The Apostles followed in the same line and were careful not to give unnecessary offence to the Roman authorities. As we all know, St Paul said that the powers that be are ordained of God. This presentation of the Christian message has persisted through the centuries. Francis of Assisi never criticised flagrant public abuses and restricted himself to guidance on personal conduct. Savonarola showed tremendous courage in criticising the papal excesses of his day and in endeavouring to apply Christian principles to the political and social issues of 15th century Italy. Who has been regarded throughout the centuries as more Christ-like – St Francis or Savonarola?

The degree of emphasis placed on political, social and economic issues raises profound questions about the purpose of life. What is the chief end of man? Archbishop Fisher caused a furore some years ago when he said in an unguarded moment that, as life on earth was a brief affair and a better life lay ahead in eternity, the mass destruction of a nuclear holocaust merely hastened for the Christian a transition to a better state that was inevitable sooner or later. A first century Christian would probably have agreed with these sentiments. A 20th century Christian is horrified. Is it because he has no convinced belief in the after-life and does not see this life as a brief testing time for eternity? Are we in the position of orthodox Jews in Christ's time when it was not an article of faith to have any settled view about what happened after death – the Sadducees believed one thing and the Pharisees another? There are few references to an after-life in the Old Testament and it is noticeable how fond of Old Testament texts are those who urge the Churches to express strong opinions on material conditions. This may be your only life: make the best of it.

Emphasis on the remedying of material conditions tends to suggest that individuals are the creatures of their environment – if conditions are bad, the individual cannot be expected to be good, if conditions are improved the individual will improve. This is the basis of the charge, so much resented by Church leaders, that they are adopting a humanist, if not a Marxist philosophy. But if the Church insists on the paramount need for material improvements and does not seem to realise that an individual can, by God's grace, rise above his environment, then is it surprising that the charge is made? We must not over-react to Marx's jibe that religion is the opiate of the people. In being anxious to show that we, too, are concerned about material conditions, we must not fall into the error of making material conditions all-important.

The Archbishop of Canterbury's Commission on Urban Priority Areas was very anxious to establish that the Church should make strong representations on Government policy towards the poor. It laid itself open to the charge of having a very materialistic view of Christ's teaching. Thus it said:

Where unemployment, poor housing and the threat of criminal violence have reached such proportions that they are like a disease, they so dominate people's thinking and feeling that no presentation of the gospel is possible which does not relate to these material deprivations. In these circumstances, everything tells against the notion that there is 'soul', quite independent of social and economic conditions, to which an entirely personal gospel may be addressed.[1]

The Very Revd Dr G T H Reid welcomed the report as a wonderful presentation of the Gospel.[2] Others may think that it is a distorted and wholly inadequate presentation of what Christ can do for all, whatever their physical circumstances. Moreover minimum material needs is a relative term – relative to the prevailing general standards. What was accepted a hundred years ago without complaint would be regarded now as unacceptable. Are we to regard receptiveness to Christ's message as going up and down like a yo-yo, depending on national material standards?

One trouble about *Faith in the City* is that it never seems to consider the effect of the report on those with whom it is concerned. Not very flattering to them! In laying such emphasis on what public authorities should do, it proceeds on the basis that the individual has rights. He has, but the Christian message is concerned with duties not rights. As has been said in another context, what we need is not a Bill of Rights but a Declaration of Duties. The Chief Rabbi, Sir Immanuel Jakobovits, published a Jewish view on *Faith in the City* which provided a much needed corrective. He emphasised the need for developing self-respect and self-help in the inhabitants of inner cities and the need to build up home life, with its closely-knit duties, as 'the inner fortress of love, care, decency and every social virtue' and 'the principal haven against exposure to the bitter realities of life outside'.

It is easy to fall into the trap of regarding the State as possessing limitless resources and of joining the queue of suppliants for State assistance for this or that cause. This develops the wrong relationship between Church and State.

There are obviously current issues on which the Church is entitled to express views – the social evils of large-scale unemployment and the wickedness of any 'I'm all right, Jack' attitude by those in employment, the threat of nuclear war, the need for measures to counter child abuse and to prevent the exploitation of the young by drug-pushers, excessive drinking and gambling, the preservation of the Christian Sunday. But from such issues, broadly treated, one moves to issues where there is no easy agreement, especially on the specific measures to be taken. One thinks of Scottish self-government or monetarism in financial policy. In the 1983 Assembly, the Very Revd Dr J G Matheson drew attention to the danger that controversial views expressed by the Church and Nation Committee could upset the harmonious climate in which the Assembly deliberations on matters affecting the essential work of the Church should take place.

When the Churches go beyond expressing their concern about social evils and proceed to indicate specific remedies that should be adopted, a whole range of difficult problems present themselves.

Public authorities are subject to compulsions that do not make it easy for them or their members to apply Christian principles in the form that an individual would be expected to do. A Christian is expected to be unselfish, but that is the sacrifice of his own interest. The concept is not easily applied to public authorities. Lord Hugh Cecil, a devout Christian, once put it 'No one has the right to be unselfish with other people's interests'. A trade union feels compelled to press for higher pay when this may be contrary to the national interest and when a Christian trade unionist might wish to waive his personal claim in the national interest. Public authorities faced with wrong-doing may show compassion but it is not in their power to forgive, since the wrong has been perpetrated against individuals. All this was worked out, long ago, by Reinhold Niebuhr in *Moral Man and Immoral Society* and other books. In 1934 and on other occasions, the General Assembly recognised 'the principle of the lawful employment of force upon just occasion, as an instrument for the restraint of wrong and the preservation of right and freedom in the world'. At the same time the Assembly recognised that, in the event of war, conscience enlightened by the Holy Spirit must decide the individual's course of action. Lord Attlee, in his staccato way, saw the matter similarly when he said of unilateral nuclear disarmament 'Non-resistance is not a political attitude. It is a personal attitude. I do not believe that it is a possible policy for people with responsibility.'[3]

A public authority may adopt a long-term policy likely to

benefit most of the people in the long run but involving temporary hardship to some in the short-term. If the Church raises its voice against the hardships (as it tends to do), it lays itself open to the retort that fools and bairns should not see things half done.

It is right to ask public authorities and other organisations to act justly, but in view of the compulsions under which they operate they have often to be controlled by the restriction of their powers, not by appealing to their better natures. Certain courses of action may have to be absolutely forbidden. If the Churches enter this field, the danger is that they become infected with the virus of compulsion and fail to show Christian compassion. A good example of this – dare one mention it – is in the general attitude of the Churches to the South African Government. The Afrikaaner people have inherited a terrible legacy and are faced with agonising choices. They are almost certainly sincere in their belief that a black majority would result, sooner rather than later, in a communist regime – atheist, ruthless, inefficient and corrupt. The attempt to engage in dialogue – reproachful dialogue – with the white Dutch Reformed Churches is less and less in evidence, even among the churches that share their Calvinist and presbyterian background. The World Council of Churches applies itself solely to devising policies designed to harm the South African Government, without a trace of Christian compassion for the Afrikaaner people or any apparent interest in the bloodshed and chaos that its policies would cause.

These are some of the difficulties about the Church lecturing public authorities on their duties and indicating specific policies that should be adopted. The Church is not likely to have the expertise to handle the case for and against some complex solution to a complex problem. Nor do its procedures provide the kind of cut-and-thrust which is needed to ensure that every facet of a proposed course of action is thoroughly examined. The Church does not always appear to advantage when its views are subjected to public examination and analysis before some tribunal or in the Press.

When it comes to suggesting or supporting specific remedies for political or economic problems, Church committees labour under disadvantages which they do not always seem to realise sufficiently. They lack expertise in the subjects they profess to deal with. Their remedies, if original, are not subject to the critical examination which is required – they do not have the buffeting to which proposals made by political parties are normally subjected before adoption. The tendency, as Bishop Newbigin has pointed out, is for much Christian speaking and writing on public issues to be based more on currently popular ideologies than on Scripture and the Christian creeds.[4] If they simply put forward remedies suggested by a political party, it is doubtful if they are adding much and they cause contention and disagreement within the Church.

There is a great need to think out afresh the manner in which the Church expresses views on public issues and the precise significance to be attached to the expression of these views.

The organisation of the Church is designed to enable *decisions* to be reached on matters within the province of the Church, if necessary by majority vote. This is clear and well-understood. Here the Church is exercising power and can impose its will within its own community.

When the Church, or a committee of the Church, expresses an opinion on a non-spiritual issue, possibly by a majority vote, quite different considerations arise. Committees and individuals who pontificate on issues, explicitly or implicitly in the name of the Church, need to examine carefully on what basis they are acting. They ought really to say that the secular authorities may be interested to know that a certain opinion was held by all or a majority of the members who happened to vote at a meeting of the Church body or of one of its committees. As regards the effect on members of the Church the position is more difficult. Is the Church saying that it believes that it is indicating God's will on the issue? Is a member of the Church who holds a contrary view and acts on that contrary view sinful and deserving of censure? Surely not. He is entitled to form his own opinion about the application of Christian principles to the matter in hand.

The ordinary man does not always clearly distinguish between the exercise of authority by the Church and the expression of opinion. The expression of a foolish or perverse opinion casts doubts on the soundness of action by the same authorities in spiritual matters. Churches should always think carefully before expressing views on political, social or economic affairs, lest they undermine their authority on matters clearly within their province.

Many of the problems involved in the handling of social, political and economic issues by the Church can be illustrated from recent experience in the Church of Scotland.

The Church and Nation Committee of the General Assembly was set up in 1920, as a means of formulating and expressing the Church's concern, on moral and social grounds, about current trends in the life of the nation.

In the early years the committee dealt with subjects that would now be regarded as within the province of other committees – should ordination wait for election to a charge, competitive preaching in filling charges, superintendence of congregations by presbyteries and so forth. Where it dealt with public issues it did so in a broad way and did not enter into detailed remedies. It dealt in this way with subjects such as gambling, the problems of depopulated rural communities, and mixed marriages. It was robust on Irish immigration, saying (1924) that the immigrant population was not being assimilated to any great degree by the native population. 'Hence a nation within a nation and the immigrant native manifests very marked contrasts in social and moral conduct and ideals with the native Scottish population.' It returned to this problem in 1925 – 'The outlook for the Scottish nationality is such as to fill the minds of all thoughtful people with grave anxiety and alarm'. No reference to the delights of ecumenical contacts. In 1928 the Committee expressed concern about serious unemployment among miners. 'It is not our province as churchmen to discuss the economics of the situation but we are under obligation to keep in the forefront the human relations and flesh and blood factors of the problem'.

After the Second World War, the Committee continued to draw attention to serious social problems while leaving the responsible authorities to find the remedies. The subjects treated in this way included rural depopulation (1948), housing and overcrowding (1949 and 1950) and the herring and white fish industries (1950). It dealt at length with the nuclear threat but rejected unilateral disarmament (1947). It disliked the centralisation of control in nationalised industries and favoured greater devolution of authority (1947). On South Africa and Southern Rhodesia (now Zimbabwe), the Committee said:

> The fears of the white population – which after all achieved much of the prosperity and development of these territories – are very real and definite .... It is well to restate that the policy of Great

Britain is to seek the fullest welfare and freedom of the native population, but the way is neither simple nor easy (1948).

On Communism, the Committee said:

There are those who do not want the Christian church to become identified with the forces of reaction .... But they are servile or recreant if they blind us to the malignancy of the threat to Christian institutions and to human liberty and dignity. The past failures of the Church will not be redeemed by a much more shameful failure now (1949).

The Committee said that there was much discussion and disagreement on the Church's attitude to war, but that in such a situation it was well to remember that the *Westminster Confession of Faith*, the Church's subordinate standard, states that the civil magistrate may lawfully wage war upon just and necessary occasions (1950).

The reports often concentrated on action within the province of the Church. For example, in 1946, in relation to the serious post-war housing situation, the Committee asked ministers and elders to make a study of the problem as it affected their own parishes and to pass on to their congregation the sense of urgency which this study would awake, also to prepare people for the cost burden which better housing provided by public authorities would entail.

What is noticeable, in comparing these reports with present day reports, is the present tendency of the Committee to express views on a great variety of topics, at home and abroad, including topics (notably abroad) on which the Committee can have no direct knowledge or experience and to go beyond drawing attention to social problems by pressing specific courses of action on public authorities. There is little doubt that a strong influence behind this has been the World Council of Churches, the British Council of Churches and other inter-church organisations. There is a danger that the Church becomes unduly influenced by opinions held by individuals and groups in these organisations. This can best be illustrated by specific examples.

Falkland Islands
On 2 April 1982 Argentine armed forces invaded and occupied the Falkland Islands. This was unprovoked aggression and an-

nexation for purely territorial reasons. All the inhabitants of the Islands wished to remain British and were opposed to transfer to Argentine rule. On 5 April the first British warships sailed from Portsmouth and the Task Force was quickly built up. South Georgia was recaptured on 25 April. British troops landed on the Falklands and on 14 June the Argentine forces surrendered.

The Church and Nation Committee put in a special report to the 1982 General Assembly. The report expressed no view on Government policy but merely commended 'all measures towards a lasting and peaceful solution'. The Assembly by a majority supported the Government's handling of the crisis.

The Church and Nation Committee dealt with the matter more fully in its report to the 1983 Assembly. One might have expected that the Committee would have related the subject to the past expressed views of the Assembly. The critical attitude of the World Council of Churches to the concept of the just war in the context of the atomic bomb, had led the 1949 Assembly to appoint a special commission which reported in 1951. The commission reported that 'we believe that, if a Christian nation is faced with the terrible choice of allowing aggression, tyranny and lawlessness to triumph or of entering upon war in defence of a free and ordered society, the resort to arms may be considered legitimate and just.' The 1951 Assembly accepted the report and found no reason to depart from the received teaching that Christians may lawfully wage war upon just and necessary occasions. Again, as recently as 1982, in the Polish context, the Church and Nation Committee secured Assembly approval for the need to uphold the rights of self-determination. Under Third World influences, the United Nations had chosen to regard the British possession of the Falklands as a relic of colonialism, notwithstanding that the islands were virtually uninhabited when Britain took them over, and had refused to regard the islanders as entitled to self-determination. On would have thought that there was material to lead the Church and Nation Committee to pause, but instead it chose to model its report very largely on the standpoint of the World Council of Churches. The director of the WCC, in documents published by the WCC[5] expatiated at great length on the misjudgments made in London and Buenos Aires before the Argentine invasion, said that the British Government and media had created a war hysteria in the name of national pride and honour and described the conflict as a peculiarly unnecessary war. The Church and Nation Committee elaborated on the errors, as they saw the matter, made by the British Government, as though this mitigated the wickedness of the Argentine invasion or would have justified inaction by the Government after the invasion had taken place. The victory was described as having 'exacerbated, rather than removed, the cause of the conflict' – no reference to the fact that an act of aggression by a ruthless dictatorship had been undone and, if not thwarted, it might well have been copied by others elsewhere, with the probability of further bloodshed.

The Church and Nation Committee, without reference to dates, said that 'one of the first responses by Argentine church leaders was to get in touch with British church leaders to communicate their distress over the outbreak of hostilities'. *The Times* of 10 April 1982 reported an earlier response when Cardinal Juan Carlos Aramburu told crowds in a Good Friday procession in Buenos Aires that they were living in a historic moment, their troops in the Falklands were heroes and they were reclaiming their nation's land. What the Church and Nation Committee did not explain was that this approach by church leaders was not made until 21 April 1982, by which time it was clear that the UK Government was prepared, if necessary, to remove the invaders by force. Hostilities, in World Council of Churches and Church and Nation Committee terms, did not occur when the Argentine dictatorship invaded the Falklands but when the British Government showed itself prepared to throw them out. The 1983 Assembly was invited to agree that regard should be had to the interests but not the wishes of the Falklanders. The Assembly had to add to its deliverance something that was conspicuously lacking in the Church and Nation report – an expression of appreciation of the restraint, courage, devotion to duty and compassion displayed by members of HM Armed Forces during the Falklands conflict.

In 1986 the Church and Nation Committee again denied the rights of the Falklanders to self-determination. In the meantime a small delegation from the British Council of Churches had visited the Falklands and had obviously been somewhat sobered down on discovering how determined the Falklanders were to remain British and how strong were their feelings against becoming part of Argentina. The result was that the Assembly deliverance was in less strong terms than the committee had proposed. The episode is a reminder, among other things, that, if the Church feels obliged to express views on events at the other end of the world, the discovery of the facts on which to form a sound judgment can be difficult and expensive.

The 1983 General Assembly of the Free Church of Scotland – untrammelled by WCC connections – echoed what were probably the views of a majority of Church of Scotland members when it said in its Loyal Address:

> We give thanks to God that your Majesty and His Royal Highness Prince Philip were sustained through this past year of very great stress especially during the time of hostilities in the Falklands, when your Majesty and His Royal Highness had to bear the great burden of daily anxiety for the armed forces of the Crown and the added burden of parental concern for the safety of His Royal Highness Prince Andrew. Especially do we thank God for the many proofs of His divine favour to our nation during the campaign. We bless God who fortified the hearts of our brave armed forces to overcome such appalling conditions and gain such a victory as to excite the admiration of the world. We grieve along with your Majesty over the loss of life and the cruel injuries suffered by so many of our troops as the price paid for resisting aggression and upholding the cause of freedom.

Aid for Third World

There is general agreement among Christians that more should be done to lessen the great disparity between the living standards of the wealthier parts of the world and the living standards of the great majority of the populations of the Third World. There is, however, no agreement how it can best be achieved.

Some Third World governments are corrupt and relatively indifferent to the living standards of the poorer of their peoples. In many cases, there is no certainty, and in some cases no probability, that foreign aid will be used to better the lot of the mass of the people. Funds made available may be used in grandiose projects. Nor is there any agreement how aid which is properly applied can best be used to raise standards of living.

Nevertheless the Church and Nation Committees repeat endlessly the views of the international organisations that a rising percentage of our GNP should be devoted to foreign aid through Government subvention. This means that a church member who gives generously to voluntary agencies operating in the

Third World is being told that he ought to be taxed to provide Government aid, even though he may consider that assistance to Governments is inefficient.

This is another case where the main thrust should be to the Church's own members, to give more to various voluntary schemes, leaving the more difficult problems of Government aid to be expressed in general terms.

Constitutional questions

Although it is now some time since representatives of the Church and Nation Committee gave evidence before the Royal Commission on the Constitution (1969–1973), their evidence raised points of abiding interest. Evidence before a Royal Commission is published and is available for all to read. The Commission was set up to consider whether there should be changes in the present functions of Parliament and Government in the United Kingdom – that is, whether Scotland and Wales should have a measure of self-government.

Dr E George Balls (convener) and Dr William B Johnston (vice-convener) with two other representatives appeared for the Church and Nation Committee. The paper submitted said that Scottish self-government had been the concern of the Church and Nation Committee and of the General Assembly for more than 20 years. Legislative freedom for Scotland within the framework of the United Kingdom would improve the Scottish economy, reduce emigration from Scotland, and enable Scotland to make a distinctive response to the idea of closer European unity.

Under examination by the members of the Commission much of this fell to pieces, notwithstanding the declared 20 years study by the Church. The witnesses could give no clear account of the extent of the legislative devolution that they wanted. As one member of the Commission said 'I do not think it is good enough to put forward proposals that in some respects are inconsistent and then to say "We are not experts in this matter." This is not an expert matter. It is a question of deciding how far you want to go'. Then Commissioners pointed out the dilemma which the Church had failed to face. If Scotland was to remain in the framework of the United Kingdom, with a common currency, no tariff barrier, no passports and free movement of capital – if in other words the UK was to remain basically a single economic and political unit – then Scotland could not have the freedom to do all the things the Church suggested. 'If you remain in the United Kingdom, many things in the United Kingdom will have to be decided by a majority of the inhabitants of the United Kingdom.' Moreover, the Irish Republic have not found that independence reduces Irish emigration. The Treaty of Rome required signatories to be treated as entities and gave no chance of a distinctive Scottish response. On statistics, the Church representatives floundered (as most of us do), being unable to explain why the existing statistics were inadequate or what they wanted or what they were trying to prove.

In response to a question, the convener demurred at the suggestion that the Church was primarily engaged in mission (a revealing attitude) and preferred to say that it was 'witnessing the Gospel'. Asked whether under the proposals the Church's position would be better he said 'I do not think that this is an element which has entered into our calculations at all. We have put forward these suggestions not in the interests of the Kirk but in the interests of the Scottish people'. As the Church and Nation Committee were engaged on so entirely secular a task, it is perhaps unfair to upbraid them for failing to draw the Commission's attention to the sovereignty of the Church of Scotland in spiritual matters. But it should have interested a body examining the British constitution. It might have prevented the Commission from making statements in their report which seemed to accept the English concept of parliamentary sovereignty in all matters. Spiritual independence, formally accepted in the Church of Scotland Act, 1921, was won at a great price over the centuries and should be asserted on all proper occasions.

One member of the Commission wanted to send back the Church and Nation Committee to do their homework again and to appear before the Commission with more precise proposals. However the Chairman (Lord Crowther) seemed to have had enough and said diplomatically that the purpose of the session had been 'to bring out the strength, and maybe the weaknesses, of the case you have put before us'.

The Church and Nation Committee is still pressing the case for Scottish self-government, and in 1987 asked for a referendum on 'devolution'. A referendum would have to be precise about what was at issue, and there is no sign that the Committee has any clearer idea what it wants.

Gartcosh

On 8 August 1985 the Government announced that the British Steel Corporation was to close down its steel cold-rolling mill at Gartcosh. This caused deep concern in Scotland because of the loss of employment and because it seemed to add to the risk that the steel works at Ravenscraig would be closed down at a later date. There was a great volume of protest from all quarters but no sign that the Government and the Corporation were prepared to yield.

The Church and Nation Committee authorised its convener to write a letter which *The Times* published on 11 November 1985. The letter argued that Gartcosh had won export markets which would be lost, that the British Steel Corporation had already cut its steel-making capacity more than its European partners and that Gartcosh should be retained to cope with demand when there was an upturn in the economy. In effect the Committee were saying that the Corporation had reached the wrong decision on economic grounds, with the inference that the Church and Nation Committee knew better how to run the steel industry. A Scottish Conservative MP wrote to *The Times* a few days later saying that the letter was remarkable for its ignorance and inaccuracy. Whatever the merits of the arguments, one is troubled whether the Church and Nation Committee should have entered into the controversy on non-spiritual terms. However unpalatable the thought may be, the truth is that a letter in these terms would just be added to the pile of other protests on the subject. The Church is a sovereign authority. Its committees should be cautious about placing themselves and the Church in the position of being rebuffed and to some extent humiliated on a non-spiritual basis.

Conclusion

The Church needs to remember the message of Professor T P Torrance in *Life and Work* of April 1981:

> The primary emphasis of Christ and of the whole New Testament message is upon salvation. Yet that is the very note that has gone out of our preaching and Church instruction. Of course salvation includes the whole man. But are we not now so mesmerised by the element of 'holy materialism' in the Christian message that we have shifted the centre of our preaching and teaching away from justification by grace to justification by social righteousness?

What would Calvin and Knox, not to mention St Paul, who were no less concerned with personal and social righteousness, say to the Church of Scotland today? In our obsession with making the Church relevant we seem to have reduced preaching to being the servant of public opinion, indeed the opinion of a permissive society, and tend to lose the transforming, revolutionary power of the Cross of Christ which alone can save society. The 'could kail het again' of the preaching 'do-gooders' has been counter-effective, for it has bored and nauseated multitudes of people who can no longer stomach the institutional Church. Somehow the Church, concerned with projecting its own image, has got in the way of Christ, but it is Christ for whom the people hunger.

As Bishop Newbigin points out,[6] a church acting corporately is probably wise to confine its official pronouncements on public questions to a limited range of matters where great ethical issues are at stake. It is well advised in many cases to go no further than to express its concern about a certain situation, to express the hope that measures will be taken to remedy the shortcomings and to give guidance to its own members. Archbishop Temple, than whom no one had a keener sense of the need to correct injustices, said that it was for the Church to indicate the Christian principles that should guide those who act in the public sphere but that the Church did not have the knowledge to indicate the right courses to take in economic matters.

A good test for Assembly Committees which are contemplating public statements on political and economic affairs is – in making this pronouncement do we believe that we are setting out God's will, as we see it? The very useful reports prepared in the last war were called *The Interpretation of God's Will in the Present Crisis*; not a bad test!

Notes and references to Chapter VI

1 Archbishop of Canterbury's Commission on Urban Priority Areas (1985). *Faith in the City*. Church House Publishing, p51.
2 *The Scotsman*, 5 December 1985.
3 Rowse, A L (1985). *Glimpses of the Great*. Methuen, p57.
4 Newbigin, Leslie (1984). *The Other Side of 1984*. World Council of Churches, p38.
5 Commission of the Churches on International Affairs (1983). Documents on the Falklands/Malvinas Crisis.
6 Newbigin, Leslie (1984). *Op. cit.*, p41.

Summing-up

The Christian faith is too many-sided to be confined in one mould. Its richness and diversity and its capacity to appeal to all races, all types and all ages can come to full fruition only if it is free to grow in different forms within the essential substance of the faith.

Judaism was tolerant of variations in the presentation of its faith, as was Christianity in its early years. The spectacular spread of Christianity in the first century took place while Christians displayed a wide variety of beliefs and organisation. An ardent faith in Christ as Lord and Saviour was the over-riding belief which held the community together. This faith enabled Christianity to survive when it might have vanished as a separate force and its members fallen back into Judaism or into ideologies, like gnosticism, which endeavoured to graft Christian features on to paganism.

The attempt to clamp the whole Church into one regimented organisation has not succeeded in the past and will not succeed in the future. In mediaeval times, the main breach was between the Western and Eastern Churches and then there was the mighty explosion of the Reformation. The ecumenical movement is backward looking, not only in its attempt to deal with old problems by means of an old form of organisation, but also in its failure to face the facts of the existing situation. We are moving into a period of diversity, when indigenous churches in America, Africa and Asia are feeling their way to forms of Christianity that meet their own needs. It is becoming more and more apparent that the strength of the Christian faith will be in the variety of its appeal. Evangelicals concerned to extend the bounds of the Kingdom will burst any ecclesiastical fetters that are imposed. The ecumenical movement in the narrow form which it has taken is operating against the tide and is failing. We need now to think, not of the so-called sins of our divisions, but of the glory of a spiritual unity which accepts diversity in doctrine and organisation. We must always ensure the fundamental unity of the Christian community by close collaboration with fellow-Christians and common endeavours. All the longings for unity should be poured into these channels and not into vain searches by ecclesiastics for elaborate institutional amalgamations.

Christians in Scotland, whatever their denomination, desire to further Christ's kingdom in Scotland. The idea that this task can be effected by the contriving of an elaborate organisation in place of the existing churches is a delusion.

For too long, the members of the Church of Scotland have remained on the defensive against the attempts of the ecumenists to impose on the Church the three-tier ministry, the exaltation of the sacraments at the expense of the Word and other features of an ecclesiastically dominated regime. The time has come to put all this on one side. Instead, let us awake to the real challenges of the times and seize our opportunities. In the presbyterian organisation of the Church of Scotland we have a marvellous instrument that can be further developed for the expansion of Christ's Kingdom. In this task the Church of Scotland has the great asset of the loyalty which its presbyterian constitution has enabled it to evoke from its members. We need, by every means in our power, to enhance the sense of responsibility of the ordinary member, so that he wishes to play his full part in the evangelisation of Scotland. Just as in 1638 the eldership sprang to life through being given more power and more responsibility, so now today we need to give more responsibility to members and to encourage elders to play their full part in the courts of the Church. The spirit of 1638 needs to be applied to this wider task. Awake, my fellow-presbyterians, awake.

Appendix

Statement of belief

The Bible

1 The supreme and final source of truth in all that concerns God's relations to man and his purpose for them is the Lord Jesus Christ. In Jesus Christ, His Son, God has once and for all made himself known to men for their salvation.

2 God makes this saving truth known to men through the Bible. The 39 books of the Old Testament and the 27 books of the New Testament were inspired by God and contain all essential knowledge on the nature of God, on the purpose of man's life and on his faith and his salvation. The Bible has unique authority because it is the inspired record and interpretation of God's supreme act of self-giving and self-disclosure in Jesus Christ. The history of ancient Israel, as interpreted by the prophets, the fulfilment of that history in Jesus Christ and the creation of the Church of Jesus Christ by the Holy Spirit, disclose and exhibit God's character and purpose, his love and saving power. All this the Bible sets forth in written words, so that through it, and the enlightenment afforded by the Holy Spirit, men are confronted afresh in every generation with Christ, the living Lord, and find God speaking to them in Him.

3 Subsequent manifestations of belief and subsequent religious practices have to be tested always by the mind of Christ, as disclosed in the Bible. The Scriptures convey the counsel of God on all matters necessary for faith and life for all who study them under the guidance of the Holy Spirit. The authority of the Scriptures does not depend on their verbal inerrancy nor on their apparent accuracy in all particulars, as judged by current historical or scientific knowledge.

God

4 There is one living and true God, infinite and eternal. He is beyond the comprehension of man, save in so far as he has

123

revealed himself through Jesus Christ to be most loving, merciful, long suffering, abundant in goodness and truth, forgiving iniquity, the rewarder of them that diligently seek him, but hating all sin and most just and to be feared in his judgments.

5 In the unity of the Godhead, there are three persons, of one substance, power and eternity – God the Father, God the Son and God the Holy Spirit. The Father is of none, neither begotten nor proceeding: the Son is eternally begotten of the Father: the Holy Spirit eternally proceeds from the Father and the Son.

Man

6 God made all things, visible and invisible. He created out of nothing the universe and all that it contains, and the universe is but a partial expression of the infinite glory and majesty of his eternal being. He is above all his works and in them all, upholding them and guiding their course. Nothing is beyond his knowledge and control. He is not to be regarded as subject to space or time.

7 God gave men reason and moral and spiritual insight that they could know him and hear his call. He gave them power of choice so that, as responsible persons, they could serve him in willing obedience and trust. Yet all men are sinful in that to a greater or lesser degree they give effect to their own desires and purposes, and withhold from God the complete love and obedience to which he is entitled. No man can blame others for his sins or ascribe them to the working of forces outside himself. Nor can God be held responsible for sin. Men, being sinners, are guilty before God and unable to save themselves.

Salvation Through Christ

8 God came into human life in Jesus Christ – the eternal Son of God made flesh. In Jesus, God became in nature one with man, being tempted like man, yet without sin. In his death on the Cross Christ, in obedience to the Father's will, freely identified himself with sinful man and offered himself for the sins of sinful but redeemable man. By this act of personal obedience and love, he made atonement for sin, won the victory over it and broke the power of evil in the world. God vindicated this sacrifice and confirmed this victory by raising Christ from the dead, thus overcoming for man the tyranny of death and proclaiming in this act of grace the final triumph of his holy love.

9 The love of God is not bestowed on a man as a reward, since none can deserve it, nor is it withheld for his sinfulness, else none could receive it. A man is saved only by the redeeming act of God in Christ.

10 God chooses those who will be saved for eternal life, though in human terms the occasion and timing of this salvation are hidden from us.

11 Those whom God chooses he reconciles to himself, not by infusing righteousness into them but by pardoning their sinfulness.

12 Such as truly believe in Jesus Christ and love him in sincerity, endeavouring to walk in all good conscience before him, may be reasonably assured that they are in a state of grace and may rejoice in the hope of the glory of God. Their faith is the sole instrument, on the human side, of reconciliation with God, being justification by faith. They may, nevertheless, by their sins fall under God's fatherly displeasure and not have his confidence restored to them until they humble themselves, confess their sins, beg pardon and renew their faith and repentance.

13 The manner in which Christ's redemption operates in the case of those who have never heard the Scriptures is hidden from us.

The Church

14 The Invisible Church is the community in heaven and earth of those who, being united with God by faith, are reconciled to him.

15 The Visible Church – Catholic or Universal – consists of all those, together with their children, who confess their faith in God and profess obedience to him. There are many branches of the Universal or Catholic Church, differing in doctrine, in tradition and in circumstances; yet through the union of all its true members with Jesus Christ the Church is one. The boundaries of the true Church cannot be determined by man and are known to God alone.

16 The Lord Jesus Christ is the only head of the Church and to his will alone is it subject. He is the sole mediator between God and man.

17 The vocation of the Church is joyfully to bear witness to its Lord, to worship God in his name, to build up its members in faith and righteousness and the spirit of unity, to proclaim his

gospel to the ends of the earth, to give loving service to mankind for his sake and to watch, pray and work for the coming of his kingdom.

Spiritual Independence of the Church

18 The Church, as part of the Universal Church, wherein the Lord Jesus Christ has appointed a government in the hands of Church office-bearers, receives from him, its divine king and head, and from him alone, the right and power, subject to no civil authority, to legislate and to adjudicate finally, in all matters of doctrine, worship, government and discipline in the Church.

The Ministry

19 The organisation of a church in the manner indicated below is agreeable to the Word of God.

20 Every member of the Church has his place and ministry. He is called to some form of service, according to the measure of Christ's gifts to him.

21 Those set apart for spiritual duties in the ministry are preaching elders (or ministers) and ruling elders.

22 A minister is chosen by a congregation and is ordained to preach the Gospel, administer the sacraments and to give pastoral care and oversight to the members of his congregation. He participates, as required, in the work of the higher courts of the Church.

23 Ruling elders assist a minister in pastoral care and oversight of the members of the congregation. They are members of the Kirk Session, and when elected to the higher courts of the Church have equal right with ministers to discuss and vote in all matters, including doctrine, worship and discipline as well as the general work of the Church. This right does not include the imposition of hands at the ordination of ministers, the pronouncement of sentences of excommunication and absolution and the intimation of sentence and censure relating to ministers.

Worship

24 Religious worship is not tied to any place or any day. God is to be worshipped everywhere – each one by himself, in families and in public assemblies.

25 The first day of the week is the Lord's Day, set apart for the worship of God.

The Word

26 By his grace God conveys faith through the Holy Spirit into the mind and heart of man and this is ordinarily wrought by the word and the preaching of the word and by prayer, by which also and by the administration of the sacraments faith is increased and strengthened.

The Sacraments

27 The two sacraments – Baptism and the Lord's Supper – were instituted by Christ at God's appointment to set forth in symbolic form the redemptive work of Christ and they are means through which God imparts his grace. The sacraments effect a visible difference between those that belong to the Visible Church and the rest of the world. Their benefits are received by faith and by them faith is quickened and confirmed. They are not to be separated from the proclamation of the gospel.

Baptism

28 In the sacrament of Baptism Christ receives a believer or the child of a believer into his Church. Baptism is administered with water in the name of the Father and of the Son and of the Holy Spirit, and signifies the outgoing grace of God to all who repent and put their whole trust in him, the washing away of their sin through the death of Christ, and the gift to them of newness of life in the family of God. In infant baptism the same grace is given and promised to the child of believing parents. The child is received into the Church in the confidence that, nurtured and trained in a Christian home and in the fellowship of Christ's people, he will be led by the Holy Spirit in due time to make his own profession of faith in Christ as his Saviour and Lord.

29 Although it is most desirable that all should be baptised, grace and salvation are not so inseparably annexed to it that no person can be regenerated or saved without it.

30 The sacrament of Baptism is but once to be administered to any person.

Lord's Supper

31 The sacrament of the Lord's Supper has its origin in the action of Christ at his last supper with his disciples, and his command to them to commemorate his death in like manner. By his own appointment the bread broken and the wine poured out shew forth his sacrifice on the cross. When in obedience to his

command believers gather round the table and eat the bread and drink the wine, they do so in thankful remembrance of Christ and his sacrifice upon the Cross, in faith in his real presence and in joyful hope of his coming in glory. Therein Christ's gift of himself and of all his benefits is visibly set forth and bestowed upon believers in such wise that they have communion with him and with all the faithful of God.

32 The sacrament is not to be taken lightly, but after prayer and due preparation and is effective only for those worthy to receive it. It is entirely proper to mark the solemnity of the occasion by celebration only a few times in the year.

Admission to Communicant Membership

33 When the children of believers approach the adult state, and others desire to join the Church, they should receive instruction in the substance of the faith. On profession of their faith, the Kirk Session will then admit them to full membership and to the Lord's Table.

34 It is desirable, but not essential, that an unbaptised person who makes profession of his faith with a view to communicant membership should be baptised.

Marriage

35 Marriage is to be between one man and one woman. It was ordained for the mutual help of husband and wife and for the continuance of mankind. It is to be entered upon as a life-long relationship. Divorce is justified only by adultery and by an irretrievable breakdown of marriage.

The Christian Hope

36 The Christian hope here and in the world to come is founded in Christ. God who alone can read the heart will judge all men by Christ. Wickedness will not go unpunished. Those who for their faith are chosen by God for eternal life will live in perfect fellowship with God and with one another. God has not disclosed the mode of the life hereafter but, inasmuch as it is continuous with the life now lived with him, it will be a fully personal life.

37 At the last, Christ will be manifested in the fulness of his power and glory. The eternal purpose of God will be accomplished, his kingdom will come in its fulness and he himself will be all in all.